# soup of the day

# soup of the day

### LYDIE MARSHALL

*Foreword by Calvin Trillin*

HarperCollins*Publishers*

HarperCollins books may be purchased for educational, business, or sales promotional use. For information, please write: Special Markets Department, HarperCollins Publishers Inc., 10 East 53rd Street, New York, NY 10022.

*first edition*

Designed by Ph.D

Printed on acid-free paper

Library of Congress Cataloging-in-Publication Data

Marshall, Lydie.
    Soup of the day / Lydie Marshall.
        p. cm.
    Includes index.
    ISBN 0-06-018809-X
        1. Soups. I. Title.

TX757 .M36 2002
641.8'13—dc21          2002068693

03 04 05 06 07 ❖/RRD 10 9 8 7 6 5 4 3 2 1

# FOR
## wayne
### MARSHALL,
*my soup lover*

# table OF

# contents

# acknowledgments

I want to thank all my friends and students who have contributed their favorite soup recipes for *Soup of the Day:* Lorette Noudel, Arlette Brisson, Harvey S. Shipley Miller, Susan Merrill, Josephina Recio, Osa Sommermeyer, Evelyne Lartigau, Cecily Brownstone, Alicia Campbell-Collins, Margaret Casparian, Dominique Barres, Debbie Ahern, Mary Jane O'Meara, Elfie Lloyd, Lorna and Neil Myers, Elizabeth Hertz, Giovanna Bambi, Julia Tiber, Frank Veneroso, Renée Behnke, Marchessa Spinola, Ruth Ziegler, and Patricia Fieldsteel. Inge Wilkinson and Tara Reddi were a great help testing and creating recipes with me; Sarah Lambert (thanks to whom I will continue teaching in Provence), a great teacher and a master of desserts, contributed some of the desserts in this book. My thanks also go to Arlette Vantrebout and Francoise Surrugue, my two helpers who love to cook with me, and finally to Colette Valentin and her daughter Eliane Moinier, my friends and neighbors with whom I spend hours in the kitchen talking and cooking. A big thank you to Karen Hanson who tested many of these recipes in her Connecticut kitchen. Many thanks to Joe Letscher, my computer guru who helped me so much while I wrote this book. There would not have been a book without my friend and editor Susan Friedland, who also contributed one of her favorite recipes, the Borscht. And I should thank Wayne for eating all these soups, but actually it was no hardship for him since soup is his favorite meal.

**foreword by**
*Calvin Trillin*

Since I love potatoes in every form, I was naturally appreciative when my friend Lydie Marshall wrote a potato cookbook, *A Passion for Potatoes*, published in 1992. I happen to love soup even more than I love potatoes, and, as if she had divined that, Lydie has now written a soup cookbook. The way she's moving from one of my favorites to another, I wouldn't be surprised if her next book turned out to be about beer.

When I'm staring out of an airplane window recalling dishes I particularly miss from various places I've been—I do a certain amount of that sort of thing, while other people in similar circumstances devise useful inventions or compose sonnets—I often find myself thinking of soup. Provence is strongly associated in my mind with pistou, a soup I have previously described as "bearing the same resemblance to vegetable soup that a Greek wedding celebration bears to a bridge-club tea," and the Riviera with Mediterranean fish soup, a miniature sea of rich broth spotted with succulent little toast-islands that look mountainous because of the rouille piled on them. Gumbo is at the forefront of the thoughts I have about Louisiana—oyster gumbo and andouille gumbo and okra gumbo. When I think of the time I spent in Seville some years back, I can recall the

# I love

particularly soup that is made by Lydie Marshall.

# soup

excitement of spotting a sign on a restaurant window saying "Hoy gazpacho!" In my musings, the entire borough of Queens still shimmers from the day I ate a bowl of noodle and vegetable soup called *lagman* in a kosher Uzbekistani restaurant in Forest Hills.

Any number of times, I have gone someplace with the intention of eating some non-soupy specialty and come back raving about the soup. That happened in Tuscany, which left me with a permanent craving for pappa al pomodoro and ribollita. I once went to Ecuador with the express purpose of searching out the tastiest ceviche and returned singing the praises of a traditional Holy Week dish called fanesca, a soup so time-consuming to make that I suggested as an appropriate menu name Potage Labor Intensive. My soup yearning is no respecter of station: I have an occasional yen for the chicken tortilla soup at the Mansion on Turtle Creek, a posh hotel in Dallas, and I can still taste the chowder at Gladee's Canteen, a simple beachside restaurant on the South Shore of Nova Scotia which closed years ago. I normally have a quart of the Second Avenue Deli's Mushroom and Barley soup in my freezer, just in case—the way an old hand in the British colonial service would have kept a full larder as a hedge against native uprisings.

In other words, I love soup—particularly soup that is made by Lydie Marshall. Before Lydie moved back to France to become what I have always thought of as the Viscomtesse of Nyons, we were neighbors in Greenwich Village, where for thirty years she ran a cooking school so distinguished that, according to Village scuttlebutt, there was a waiting list for people who had volunteered to do the dishes for no more recompense than the opportunity to overhear bits of instruction and perhaps have a go at the leftovers. Early every autumn, when the necessary vegetables became available, Lydie would invite us over for a bowl of pistou, usually accompanied by her potato bread. Have I missed those evenings since Lydie and her husband, Wayne, moved to Nyons? No more than the average child would miss Christmas. Fortunately, the pistou recipe is here. So is a recipe for pappa al pomodoro and ribollita and chowder and chicken tortilla soup. There are also soups I've never tried and soups I've never heard of. Considering how inventive Lydie has been about soup, in fact, I can't wait to see how she handles beer.

"**Lydie,
mange ta
soupe.**"

# introduction

I still hear my mother's voice some fifty years later telling me to eat my soup. Every day, Lydie made a face but ate her soup.

Years later I married an American from Oklahoma who (without my knowing it) was starved for soups. He did not have to hear this litany—Eat your soup; it will make you strong and healthy—from his mother. So one day when we were arguing over who to vote for in the U.S. presidential election, I promised to make soup every day *forever* if he voted for my candidate. Without a thought he promptly agreed; soup meant more to him than politics. Well, my candidate won and I started making soups.

When I told friends I was writing a book on soups, I was impressed by the enthusiastic reaction to the news. Everybody wanted to give me his or her favorite recipe—one of their mother's or grandmother's, aunt's, or cousin's. I was on the way to test over a hundred soup recipes.

We love soup for many reasons: when the weather is freezing, a good hot soup is always welcome; when we are coming down with a cold, drinking a hot vegetable or chicken broth can help make us feel better; when we want to save money for a vacation, we can eat soup, an excellent and inexpensive way to be nourished. Soups made of leftovers are so well known that in French bistros, *le potage du jour* served in the evening is a mixture of whatever was left from lunch. Sometimes, such a soup is sublime but alas never duplicated.

Stock, broth, bouillon, and soup are all one, but their role and strength of flavor differ. First, *bouillon* is the French word for "broth" and a broth is made from just vegetables, or vegetables, meat, chicken, or fish. One or a selection of these are cooked with water for several hours and then strained to become a broth of savory essence. *Stock* is a word used essentially for restaurant preparation; it is a broth to be used in sauces. And soups are generally combinations of vegetables, legumes, meat, poultry, or fish cooked once more with broth.

*Soup of the Day* starts with a chapter on broth, which can be sipped on its own or used as the base for the soups in the following chapters. I always make broth, but it takes time. If you don't want to spend the time, use a good commercial broth or bouillon cubes—they are almost as good as homemade broth.

I divided the vegetable chapter into sections for all-season vegetables, one for fall and winter vegetables, for spring, and finally for summer, with cold and hot soups. In these sections, many of the soups are interchangeable between seasons; make your own decisions.

The organization of this book is fairly arbitrary because so many ingredients are all-season. Consider the chapter groupings as just suggestions about the best time of year to serve the soups and follow your own instincts about seasonal suitability.

A few notes on my techniques. There are certain technical aspects I respect when making soups. My mother puréed her soups with a food mill, which was very practical when she made soups with potatoes, since they don't become gummy when processed this way. Nowadays, I purée my soups in a blender or food processor, or with an immersion blender, but when there are potatoes in the soup I purée it in very small batches and only for a few seconds to avoid that unattractive gummy texture. But when I need a silky texture—as in a vichyssoise, for example—I push the coarse soup through a drum sieve to smooth it out or to discard debris such as fibers, or the outer membranes of legumes that will not pulverize in either the food processor or the blender; it's a technique used by chefs. In a home kitchen, fit a fine-meshed sieve over a bowl and in small batches, force the soup through the sieve with the back of a soup spoon.

I always buy Italian plum tomatoes—*plain, not in tomato sauce* (sometimes, hard to find), which gives a metallic taste that changes the taste of the soup.

Soups can be prepared ahead of time, which is a great attraction when you are planning to serve soup for a dinner party. But remember that most soups will thicken while waiting. How often do I hear, "My split pea soup was great when I made it, then I had to dilute it with water and it did not taste as good." I answer, "Always have on hand more broth to dilute it or do not purée the soup until dinnertime."

When my soup is simmering, I am not too far from the stove. The broth must not evaporate too much; be sure it is just under the boil or over a very gentle boil, otherwise too much will evaporate.

I love garnishing soups with cream when I entertain. The amount of cream is negligible but the soup looks decorative in the bowl. I put the cream in one of those ketchup or mustard plastic squeeze bottles and drip lines or blobs à la Jackson Pollock.

Aside from cold soups, all the other soups should be served boiling hot in preheated soup plates or bowls. Sometimes I pour boiling water over the plates. Or, if the oven is empty, I warm it to 300 degrees for 5 minutes, then turn it off; I line up the plates or bowls next to each other on a cookie sheet and warm them in the oven.

Soup and bread make a happy marriage; followed by a salad and dessert, you have a feast. *Bon Appétit!*

# soup of the day

# broth

I bought a 15-quart heavy-gauge aluminum stockpot from Wear-Ever in 1970, when I started teaching cooking. It found a permanent place on one of the back burners of the stove. When I moved to Nyons, in the Drome Provençale, the stockpot came with me and found its place once more on the back burner of the new stove. If you are a soup lover and make soup often, you might consider doing the same, though 8- or 10-quart pots might suffice if you don't teach and make as many soups as I do.

I was fortunate years ago to spend a week in the kitchens of Taillevent, one of the great restaurants of France where the basic preparation of stock begins on Monday morning when they reopen after closing for the weekend. I went to work near what looked like an enormous sink but was in fact a huge stockpot built in to one of the kitchen counters. It was full of meat bones and took one hour to fill with tap water. It cooked slowly (the heating system was also built in), and periodically ends and bits of vegetables were added to the broth that was to be used as braising liquids and for the base of many of their famous sauces. The kitchen smelled heavenly.

# 1

# beef broth

Beef broth serves as a basis for lots of soups—it adds depth and structure to soups. For a flavorful beef broth, buy a large quantity of meat, a cut of beef like brisket or beef shanks that tolerate long, slow cooking. The cooked meat makes delicious salads, such as Wayne Marshall's Tossed Salad (page 136) or the Lettuce Salad with Stuffed Tomatoes (page 146).

No need to peel the vegetables—just scrub them clean.

4 pounds brisket or beef shanks, cut crosswise into two pieces

6 quarts water

1 beef bone with marrow

3 cups coarsely chopped carrots

2 celery stalks with leaves, coarsely chopped

2 large onions, split in two, stuck with 4 whole cloves

1 1/2 cups coarsely chopped celery root or parsnip

Several sprigs of fresh parsley

2 tablespoons sea salt

Place the meat and the bone in a 15-quart stockpot. Cover with water and bring to a boil slowly. Skim the scum that rises to the surface.

Add the vegetables, parsley, and salt. Reduce the heat and cook at a gentle boil, partially covered, for 4 hours.

Fit a fine-meshed sieve or a colander lined with cheesecloth over a 4-quart mixing bowl. Using a long-handled wire skimmer, remove the meat and vegetables to the strainer to drain. Reserve the meat for one of the salads mentioned in the headnote and discard the vegetables. Pour the broth through the strainer. Cool the broth to room temperature. Refrigerate for several hours; remove the fat that hardens at the top. If you're not going to use the broth within three days, freeze it. Longer refrigeration will require reboiling every three days to avoid spoilage.

# chicken broth

I have been teaching cooking for many years, and just as I keep my knives sharpened, I have chicken broth in my refrigerator or freezer. Though I recommend you do the same, if you're caught short, use commercial low-sodium chicken broth or cubes. In New York, I sometimes buy chicken broth from the Chinese restaurant across the street, which does not use MSG; if your local Chinese restaurant is not so accommodating, buy their wonton soup and ask them to hold the wontons—the broth is generally delicious.

If you make your own broth and can't find leeks or celery root, substitute two large onions for the leeks and one parsnip for the celery root. Do not peel the vegetables; just scrub them clean.

| |
|---|
| 1 4-pound chicken or chicken backs, necks, wings, etc. |
| 6 quarts plus 1 cup water |
| 3 cups chopped carrots |
| 1 medium leek, split lengthwise, washed, and chopped |
| 1 celery stalk, with leaves, chopped |
| 2 cups chopped celery root |
| Several sprigs of flat or curly parsley |
| Several sprigs of fresh thyme or 1 teaspoon dried thyme |
| 1 bay leaf |
| 2 tablespoons sea salt |

Place the chicken in a 15-quart stockpot and cover with 6 quarts of the water. Bring to a boil very slowly. When the boil is reached, skim off the scum and the fat that rises to the top. Add the remaining cup of water and return to a boil.

Add all the vegetables, herbs, and salt. Bring to a boil, reduce the heat, and cook at a gentle boil, partially covered, for 3 hours. Once in a while, with a long-handled spoon, skim the fat that rises to the top.

Fit a fine-meshed sieve or a colander lined with cheesecloth over a 4-quart mixing bowl. Transfer the chicken and the vegetables to the strainer, using a large wire skimmer. Skin and bone the chicken and reserve the meat for a soup garnish or for making sandwiches or chicken salad; discard the vegetables.

Pour the broth through the strainer or colander. Cool to room temperature. Refrigerate for several hours; remove the fat that hardens at the top. If you don't plan to use the broth within three days, freeze it. Broth refrigerated for more than three days should be reboiled to avoid spoilage.

# turkey broth

The day after Thanksgiving, I make this broth with the turkey carcass, fresh vegetables, and some of the leftover meat. The large pieces of meat I reserve for Sandwich Monte Cristo (page 171). I use the broth as a basis for all kinds of soups calling for chicken broth, but I also serve the broth as is, with the vegetables, accompanied by Tuscan Bread (page 158) or Poilane Bread (page 156) with olive oil on the side.

Turkey carcass, some leftover turkey meat, chopped up

2 cups peeled potatoes cut into eighths

3 cups 1-inch-thick slices of peeled carrots

2 medium onions, peeled and quartered

1 large garlic clove, peeled

1 tablespoon sea salt

Freshly ground black pepper

3 quarts water

Put the turkey carcass and any meat into a 6-quart heavy bottom pot with the potatoes, carrots, onions, and garlic. Sprinkle with salt and freshly ground pepper. Cover with water and bring slowly to a boil. Reduce the heat and cook at a gentle boil, partially covered, for 2 hours.

Strain the broth, turkey carcass, meat, and vegetables into a large bowl fitted with a strainer or a colander lined with cheesecloth. It should yield 2 quarts. Remove the carcass pieces and pick the meat off the bones; reserve with the vegetables. Discard the bones.

Refrigerate the broth and use it like chicken broth as a base for soups.

Alternatively, reduce the broth to 4 cups to intensify its flavor for soup. Reheat the vegetables and meat that was left on the bones and any leftover turkey in the broth. Taste and correct the seasoning with salt and freshly ground pepper.

# vegetable broth

My friend Lorna Myers makes this broth especially as a base for Zen Split Pea and Barley Soup (page 91), which Neil, her husband, brought back from his Zen meditation group in California. It is also a substitute for all the soups that require chicken broth in this book.

1 pound small turnips, cubed (2 cups)

2 medium onions, quartered, with 2 whole cloves stuck in each quarter

5 garlic cloves

4 cups sliced carrots

4 medium leeks, tough green leaves discarded, chopped (8 cups)

4 canned Italian plum tomatoes, drained and chopped

2 loosely packed cups chopped parsley

1 sprig of rosemary

2 sprigs of thyme

4 quarts water

1 ½ tablespoons sea salt

5 peppercorns

Combine all the vegetables and herbs in a 15-quart stockpot with the water. Season with the salt and add the peppercorns. Cover the pot and slowly bring the water to a boil. Simmer for 2 hours.

Remove the broth from the heat and let it cool.

Strain the broth through a fine-meshed sieve or a colander lined with cheesecloth, pushing on the vegetables to extract as much of their flavor as possible. Reserve the mashed vegetables for Leftover Mashed Vegetable Soup (below).

Let the broth cool before refrigerating or freezing for later use.

**VARIATION: Leftover Mashed Vegetable Soup**

Purée the cooked vegetables in a processor. Add enough fresh water to thin it to a soupy consistency. Bring to a boil. For each portion, add 1 tablespoon butter. Swirl the butter into the soup.

# fish broth

When I want to make a fish broth, I give my fishmonger plenty of notice to save bones and heads for me. You can tell if a fish is fresh by the eyes, which should be bright, with no thin white film over the iris. Do not use an oily fish such as salmon or bluefish. The bigger the heads, the more meat there will be, which will add flavor to the broth.

4 pounds fish heads and bones

2/3 cup mushroom stems

1 medium onion, peeled and thinly sliced (1 cup)

1 celery stalk, thinly sliced

3 or 4 celery leaves, chopped

2 sprigs of fresh thyme or
1 teaspoon dried bay leaf

5 sprigs of parsley

2 teaspoons sea salt

1/2 cup white wine, such as Chardonnay

1 tablespoon lemon juice

3 quarts cold water

Place the fish heads, bones, vegetables, spices, wine, lemon juice, and water in a 9-quart heavy-bottomed pot. Bring slowly to a boil, skimming the surface. Reduce the heat and cook at a gentle boil, partially covered, for 45 minutes.

Line a strainer with cheesecloth and fit it over a mixing bowl. Transfer the heads, bones, and vegetables to the strainer. Push on the fish bones and vegetables with the back of a large spoon or with a pestle to extract all the flavorful broth. Discard the bones and vegetables.

Refrigerate overnight or freeze for at least six weeks.

# clarified broth for a hot consommé drink

On a cold day, after a long walk in the country or skiing, I serve a hot consommé in tea cups. I also serve it at dinner parties between the first and second courses. I love to see a very cloudy homemade broth transformed into a clear amber liquid— it's miraculous.

I clarify broth with egg whites, a small amount of minced vegetables, and some lean ground beef. The vegetables and the meat are cooked to intensify the flavor of the broth; they float to the top of the broth aided by the egg white, forming a thick layer over the liquid and acting as magnet for the impurities in the broth. This vegetable-meat-egg-white layer is then discarded, revealing a limpid broth. It is a long cooking process (1 1/2 hours), and to avoid too much evaporation while cooking, use a saucepan deeper than it is wide.

1 cup minced white of leek

1/2 cup very small diced carrots

2 egg whites

4 ounces lean ground beef (2/3 cup)

2 quarts cold Beef or Chicken Broth (pages 2, 3), degreased

Combine the leek, carrots, egg white, and ground meat in a 4-quart deep saucepan. Pour in the cold broth. Turn the heat to medium and, whisking all the while, bring the broth and vegetables to a boil. It takes at least 15 minutes to come to a boil and is the most tedious part of the clarification.

When the first boil is reached, reduce the heat and cook for 1 1/2 hours just below the boil, with bubbles appearing occasionally on the surface. With a large wire skimmer, scoop out the egg white-vegetable-meat layer and strain the broth through cheesecloth.

Reheat when ready to serve, boiling hot in cups.

# *vegetable* soups

If you are a gardener, you can respect the seasons and cook according to them; however, for those of us who buy our vegetables, we can find all kinds year-round. I chose a few soups as all-season, since carrots, leeks, potatoes, onions, and salad greens—even zucchini—are always available. I put the tomato soups in this category, too, because I make them with canned tomatoes (remember to buy plain tomatoes, without tomato sauce added), except in summer and early fall when local tomatoes are available.

The rest of the chapter is organized informally by season, but use your judgment about when to make what.

# 2

# tomato soup with frozen marrow

Alexia, mother of my friend Inge Wilkinson, would make this heart-warming tomato soup when her family started a cold; however, you don't need to feel chills before try-ing it. It's even better when you feel fine to appreciate this delicious soup, topped with crumbs of frozen marrow.

I make this soup with canned tomatoes, but during tomato season, I substitute 6 pounds of peeled fresh tomatoes.

2 pounds marrow bones, sawed into 4 pieces

1 tablespoon sea salt

1 large onion, peeled and quartered

2 carrots, peeled and sliced in half lengthwise

1 celery stalk, cut in half

1 leek, white only, split in half

2 large garlic cloves

2–3 tablespoons vegetable oil

4 (28-ounce) cans Italian plum tomatoes
or 6 pounds fresh tomatoes, peeled and seeded

4 cups Chicken Broth (page 3),
Vegetable Broth (5), or a commercial broth
or bouillon cubes

Several sprigs of parsley

Freshly ground black pepper

Preheat the oven to 425 degrees.

Line a broiler pan with a double thickness of aluminum foil. Place the marrow bones in the pan and sprinkle about 1 teaspoon salt all over them. Scatter the onion, carrots, cel-ery stalk, leek, and garlic around the bones. Drizzle over the oil and roast for 45 minutes or until the bones are golden brown.

Drain the tomatoes through a sieve clamped over a mixing bowl. Reserve the liquid. Split each tomato and squeeze out the juice through the sieve, catching the juices in the reserved liquid. Discard the tomato seeds. Chop the tomatoes coarsely and add to the tomato liquid.

When the bones are roasted, let them cool before removing the marrow. Gently dislodge the marrow with the blade of a knife and place it on top of a double layer of aluminum foil. Wrap the marrow in the shape of a small sausage and freeze. Place the roasted marrow bones, vegetables, the tomatoes and tomato liquid, and the broth in a 9-quart heavy-bottomed pot. Add parsley and sprinkle with remaining 2 teaspoons salt and the freshly ground pepper. Bring to a boil, cover, reduce the heat, and cook at a gentle boil for 45 minutes.

In batches, purée the soup in a blender or food processor, or purée with an immersion blender right in the pot.

Thirty minutes before serving, remove the marrow from the freezer and unwrap.

Reheat the soup; taste and correct seasoning before serving the soup, garnished with the sliced or crumbled marrow.

# potage crecy

Crecy is a small town fifty miles northeast of Paris, where the carrots are reputed to be the best in all of France. It is my favorite soup for a dinner party. Guests rave about the taste—even those who are not too fond of carrots—but you do need a strong chicken or vegetable stock.

4 tablespoons (1/4 cup) butter

1 large onion, peeled and chopped coarsely (1 1/2 cups)

1 large garlic clove, peeled and chopped coarsely

1 small potato, peeled and sliced

4 cups sliced carrots

3 medium tomatoes, chopped (1 1/2 cups)

Few basil leaves, shredded (1/2 cup)

5 cups Chicken Broth (page 3), Vegetable Broth (page 5), or a commercial broth or bouillon cubes

2 teaspoons sea salt

1/4 teaspoon Tabasco

Freshly ground black pepper

2 tablespoons lemon juice

Melt the butter in a 6-quart heavy-bottomed pot; add the chopped onion and garlic. Cover and simmer for 5 minutes or until soft, adding a few tablespoons of water if the vegetables are in danger of burning. Stir in the potato, carrots, tomatoes, and basil. Pour 5 cups of broth over the vegetables; sprinkle with salt and freshly ground pepper. Bring to a boil, reduce the heat, and cook at a gentle boil, partially covered, for 45 minutes.

Purée the soup in the blender a small amount at a time, or in a food processor or with an immersion blender. Add the Tabasco and lemon juice.

Just before serving, you may have to thin out the soup with more broth or purée the soup at the last minute. Taste and correct seasoning before serving the soup, very hot.

# the "day after" soup

Dominique Barres, the wife of my veterinarian, and I chat often about cooking while in the waiting room of the office (with six cats I am a permanent fixture there). I was intrigued by her "green soup," a soup she makes with only green vegetables the day after—after indulging too much on foie gras, truffles, etc.—during the holidays. Since she was rather vague about quantities, I worked out the amount of vegetables needed for this easy and tasty soup. I make the soup when I feel a cold coming on or, like Dominique, if I have indulged in too much of a good thing. It takes almost no time to prepare; the soup cooks in about twenty minutes. Don't forget to warm the soup bowls—the soup is to be served very hot.

1 medium leek, including the light green leaves

$1/2$ pound zuchini

8 loose cups of lettuce (1 head)

10 sprigs of flat-leaf parsley (about 2 ounces)

2 quarts water

5 teaspoons salt

Butter (optional)

Grated Parmesan cheese (optional)

Split the leek in half to the stem and wash thoroughly under cold running water. Chop coarsely; you should have about 2 cups.

Do not peel the zucchini. Split it lengthwise twice and then cut it crosswise in 1-inch cubes (2 cups).

Stack the salad leaves and with a large knife, shred them; you should have about 4 cups loosely packed.

Chop the parsley with stems (2 cups loosely packed).

Put all the greens in a 6-quart heavy-bottomed pot and cover with a little less than 2 quarts of water. Sprinkle with salt. Bring to a boil, cover, reduce the heat, and simmer at a gentle boil for 30 minutes.

Cool slightly and purée the soup in batches in the blender or food processor, or with an immersion blender. Taste and correct seasoning. Serve boiling hot with butter and grated Parmesan on the side, if you wish.

# classic french leek and potato soup

This is the leek and potato soup that many French cooks prepare for their evening meal during the year. It is made with water, but the potatoes and leeks are braised first in butter. You can substitute olive oil for the butter—it's not as rich-tasting.

This is one of the soups where a food mill is ideal to purée the mixture. The potatoes might get gummy if the soup is puréed in a food processor or blender. If that's all you have, process the potatoes and leeks together for just a second or so, in very small quantities at a time.

When you buy leeks, pay attention to their shape; if the white is short and the greens are tough, buy more than if they are young and tender. The amount of leek is important for the soup; you need enough for 8 cups of chopped white and tender green leaves. I taught this soup in Arizona where we had to use 6 leeks, I taught the same soup in Connecticut where I used only 3 leeks!

3 to 6 leeks, depending on size

3/4 pound Russet potatoes

1 medium onion

4 tablespoons (1/4 cup) butter

2 tablespoons sea salt

Freshly ground black pepper

8 cups water

Cut the leeks lengthwise twice, and wash under cold running water to discard any dirt. Cut off all the tough green leaves. Slice the leeks; you need 8 cups.

Peel and cut the potatoes into 2-inch cubes; you need about 2 cups.

Peel and cut the onion in half. With the cut side down, cut into thin slices; you need 1 cup.

Place the butter, leeks, potatoes, and onion in a 6-quart heavy-bottomed pot. Sprinkle with salt and pepper and stir. Cover, reduce the heat, and braise for 15 minutes or until the leeks and onion are wilted, stirring once in a while and checking that nothing burns. If the vegetables stick to the bottom of the pot, add a little water.

Pour the water over the vegetables. Bring to a boil, cover, reduce the heat, and cook at a gentle boil for 45 minutes.

Gradually purée the soup in a blender or food processor, or use an immersion blender or food mill. Just before serving, reheat the soup. If the soup is made 1 or 2 hours ahead of time, it will have thickened. Thin it out with water or broth if you have some. Taste and correct seasoning. Serve in hot bowls.

# austrian potato soup

Elfie Lloyd serves this potato soup from her native Austria on very hot days in the Bahamas, where she lives now. She likes to serve the soup boiling hot!

1 pound Yukon Gold potatoes, peeled and diced (2 cups)

1 large carrot, peeled and diced (1/2 cup)

1 celery stalk, diced (1/2 cup)

1 medium onion, peeled and coarsely chopped (1 cup)

2 sprigs of fresh thyme

4 cups water

1 tablespoon sea salt

Freshly ground black pepper

1 teaspoon cornstarch

2 cups milk (whole, 2%, or 1%)

1 tablespoon butter

Several sprigs of fresh parsley, chopped

Combine the vegetables and thyme in a 6-quart heavy-bottomed pot and add the water. Stir in 2 teaspoons of the salt and grind pepper over it. Bring to a boil, cover, reduce the heat, and simmer at a gentle boil for 20 minutes or until the potatoes are tender.

Cool. In several batches, purée the soup in a blender or a food processor.

In a mixing bowl, whisk the cornstarch with the milk and pour it into the soup, adding the butter. Sprinkle with more pepper and more salt, depending on your taste.

Just before serving, reheat the soup. Serve in hot bowls and garnish each bowl with the chopped parsley.

# pappa al pomodoro
# italian tomato and bread soup

I ate this soup, years ago, in a Florentine restaurant and found it delicious, but I had to get used to this thick mass of soaked bread with tomatoes; once I tasted a mouthful, I was won over though—it was fabulous.

I eat this soup for lunch with people who love Italian food, followed by Haricots Verts with Wild Mushrooms Salad (page 141).

This recipe comes from Giovanna Bambi, a lovely Florentine lady who makes the soup all year long. When the tomatoes are in season, the soup is a must, but it can be done throughout the year with canned Italian plum tomatoes. The delicious taste does not come solely from the tomatoes but from the rich homemade broth and from the stale Tuscan bread. For this soup, I make beef broth and boil it down to concentrate the flavors.

| |
|---|
| $1/2$ cup extra-virgin Italian olive oil |
| 2 garlic cloves, coarsely chopped |
| 1 medium red onion, cut in half and finely sliced |
| $1 1/2$ pounds very ripe tomatoes, peeled, seeded, chopped (3 cups), or 1 (28-ounce) can Italian plum tomatoes |
| Large pinch of sugar |
| 1 teaspoon red pepper flakes |
| 10 fresh leaves of basil |
| 3 cups concentrated Beef Broth (page 2), or a commercial broth or bouillon cubes |
| 4 cups stale Tuscan Bread (page 158), cut into small pieces |
| Salt |
| Freshly ground black pepper |

Heat the oil in a large 4-quart pan over low heat. Add the garlic and onion and braise for 10 minutes without burning the garlic.

Meanwhile, purée the tomatoes in the food processor for 1 minute.

Add the tomatoes, sugar, red pepper flakes, and basil leaves. Raise the heat and bring to a boil, then reduce the heat and simmer for 10 minutes. Add the broth. Bring to a boil slowly, then add the bread. Season with salt and pepper. Simmer for 5 minutes, stirring occasionally to mix bread and tomatoes. Turn off the heat, cover the pan, and let stand for 1 hour.

Reheat before serving. Taste and correct seasoning.

**VARIATION: Tomato custard**

With leftover soup, beat 2 egg whites until firm and fold into the soup. Spoon into a greased Pyrex baking dish and bake for 20 minutes in a preheated 350-degree oven. Serve as a vegetable.

# onion soup

I make onion soup with several kinds of onions, a rich beef stock, homemade bread, and grated Gruyère or Appenzeller cheese from Switzerland. I mix leeks, shallots, and yellow onions, but you can choose your own onion combination. Making onion soup is also an excuse to buy pretty individual ovenproof onion soup bowls—the soup is so appetizing in them! If you have made your own beef broth, you can follow the onion soup with Wayne Marshall's Tossed Salad (page 136) or the Lettuce Salad with Stuffed Tomatoes (page 146) with the leftover beef from the broth.

4 tablespoons olive oil

6 cups sliced onions (1⅓ pounds)

1 cup sliced shallots
(approximately 6 large shallots)

2 cups sliced whites of leeks
(approximately 2 large leeks)

1 teaspoon sugar

2 teaspoons sea salt

Freshly ground black pepper

3 cups freshly grated Gruyère or Appenzeller

6 cups Beef Broth (page 2),
or a commercial broth or bouillon cubes

6 (½-inch) slices of stale Poilane
or Tuscan Bread (pages 156, 158)

Preheat the oven to 350 degrees.

Heat the oil in a large skillet, then stir in the onions, shallots, and leeks. Sprinkle with sugar, salt, and pepper. Stir the mass of onions with a wooden spoon over low heat until the onions are totally wilted and start turning a rich golden color, about 15 minutes. Onions burn easily, so watch it; if they do burn, start over again, as there is nothing worse than burned onions. You should have about 3 cups of cooked onions.

Prepare six onion soup bowls. Sprinkle 4 tablespoons cheese into the bottom of each bowl, add ½ cup cooked onions, and pour 1 cup of broth into each bowl. Cover the bowls with a slice of bread and sprinkle another 4 tablespoons cheese over each slice of bread.

Place the bowls on a cookie sheet. Bake on the middle shelf of the oven for 20 minutes or until the tops are golden brown.

Let cool slightly before eating—onions can easily burn your palate.

# onion, bread, and cheese soup

This soup is a simpler version of the famous Onion Soup (page 18). This one is generally cooked with water but of course with a broth made either with beef, chicken, or vegetables, the soup will be richer. I make this even in the summer months; it is so delicious you forget the hot weather.

3 tablespoons butter

6 cups sliced onions (1 ⅓ pounds)

2 tablespoons flour

1 large garlic clove, peeled and pureed

6 cups Beef Broth (page 2), Chicken Broth (page 3), Vegetable Broth (page 5), or water

1 bay leaf

Salt to taste

2 cups grated Gruyère

6 thin slices of Poilane or Tuscan bread (156–59)

In a 6-quart heavy-bottomed pot, melt the butter. Add the onions and cook for 5 minutes over medium high heat, stirring the onions very often so they do not burn.

Stir 2 tablespoons flour into the onions and continue cooking and stirring for another 10 minutes until the onions are golden but not browned.

Stir in the garlic. Pour the broth or water over the onions. Sprinkle with salt and add 1 bay leaf. Cover and simmer for 20 minutes.

In a large soup tureen, layer 3 slices of bread at the bottom of the pot, cover with half the cheese, then cover with the last 3 slices of bread and top with the remaining cheese. The soup can be prepared ahead of time up to this step.

When ready to serve, reheat the onion broth and when boiling hot, pour it over the bread and cheese and serve immediately.

# fall *and* winter

I chose not to separate fall and winter soups. Most of the vegetables in the market beginning in early fall are generally found during the winter. The season for wild mushrooms is fall; even though the mushroom soups I make ask for dried mushrooms, it still is nice to respect the seasons and the Fresh Mushroom Soup could be made with fresh porcini or chanterelles; the Chestnut Soup is made with canned chestnuts, but if you prefer making it with fresh chestnuts, the chestnut season is in the fall. The Kohlrabi Soup (in Chapter 5, page 126) is better made in the fall when the kohlrabi are small and sweeter than when they become more mature through the winter. For Pumpkin Soup, fresh pumpkins are best, but they are found in the markets for a short time in the fall. For the winter, there are many varieties of winter squash to replace pumpkins, like the Butternut Soup. Celery, Celery Root, and Yellow Turnips Soups are good in the fall as well as in the winter.

# fresh mushroom soup

The soup is scrumptious; the preparation is a bit of a bother, but it is worth it.

**For the Soup:**

1/2 pound white mushrooms,
cremini, or chanterelles

1 medium onion, peeled and thinly sliced (1 cup)

1/2 cup red wine (Zinfandel or Côte du Rhône)

2 cups Chicken Broth (page 3),
Vegetable Broth (page 5), or a commercial broth or
bouillon cubes

**For the White Sauce (Béchamel)**

3 tablespoons butter

2 tablespoons flour

2 cups milk (whole, 2%, or 1%), scalded

2 1/2 teaspoons salt

Freshly ground black pepper

Buttered Toast (page nnn)

**The soup:** Chop off the bottoms of all the mushroom stems and discard.

Pick out the 12 best-looking mushrooms; cut off their stems and reserve the caps for later. Coarsely chop the stems of the 12 reserved mushrooms and chop the remaining mushrooms.

In a 6-quart heavy-bottomed pot, put the onion, the chopped mushrooms, the wine, and broth. Bring to a boil, reduce the heat, and cook at a gentle boil, partially covered, for 25 minutes.

**The white sauce:** In a 3-quart heavy-bottomed saucepan, melt the butter and whisk in the flour. Gradually add the scalded milk. Cook for 10 minutes, whisking once in a while. Season with salt and pepper to taste. Set aside.

Purée the mushroom-wine-broth mixture in several batches in a blender or food processor. Whisk the mushroom soup into the white sauce, then pour the mixture back into the soup pot.

Cut the reserved mushroom caps or chanterelles into 1/4-inch-thick slices and add them to the soup. Bring slowly to a boil, poaching the sliced mushrooms. When the boil is reached, turn off the heat. Taste and correct the seasoning. (It can be prepared ahead of time, but reheat slowly to avoid toughening the mushrooms.) Serve with buttered toast.

# dried and fresh mushroom soup

This soup is very simple to make even though from the number of ingredients, it looks more complicated than it really is, and also the dried and fresh mushrooms are cooked separately. I buy Polish dried mushrooms for this soup, but it can be made with porcini or morels and any kind of fresh mushrooms.

1 1/2 ounces dried mushrooms

2 cups warm water

1 tablespoon vegetable oil

2 1/2 tablespoons butter

1 medium onion, coarsely chopped

1 carrot, peeled and sliced

1 large garlic clove, minced

1 large tomato, peeled and seeded

Few sprigs of parsley

5 cups Chicken Broth (page 3), Vegetable Broth (page 5), or a commercial broth or bouillon cubes

2 teaspoons salt

Freshly ground black pepper

1/4 cup port wine

1/2 pound fresh white mushrooms, cleaned and cut into 1/2-inch slices

1 tablespoon fresh lemon juice

2 tablespoons flour

3/4 cup heavy cream or half-and-half

Minced chives, for garnish

Soak the dried mushrooms in warm water for 1 hour. Strain the liquid through cheese-cloth or through a coffee filter and reserve. Wash the mushrooms several times under cold water to remove any sand that may cling to the stems. Chop them coarsely and reserve.

In a 6-quart heavy-bottomed soup pot, heat the oil and 1 tablespoon butter. Stir in the onion, carrot, and garlic; cook for 1 minute, then add the tomato and parsley. Continue cooking over medium heat for another 5 minutes.

Pour the mushroom water and the broth over the vegetables. Season with salt and pepper. Bring to a boil, cover, reduce the heat, and simmer for 15 minutes. Turn off the heat and discard the parsley.

Purée the soup with an immersion blender right in the soup pot or in a blender or food processor in several batches. Add the wine and the dried mushrooms. Bring to a boil; cook at a gentle boil, partially covered, for 30 minutes.

Meanwhile, melt the remaining butter in a large nonstick skillet and sauté the fresh mushroom slices over medium-high heat. Add the lemon juice and sauté another few minutes. Turn off the heat and reserve.

In a small bowl, combine the flour with the cream and pour it over the sautéed white mushrooms; stir to combine and add to the soup for the last 5 minutes of cooking. Taste and correct seasoning. Decorate each soup plate with minced chives.

# porcini consommé

For Christmas, my French friend Lorette adds diced fresh truffle to this delicious and elegant soup. I serve it for a first course at a dinner party.

3 ounces dried porcini

3 cups warm water

3 tablespoons butter

3 tablespoons all-purpose flour

6 cups Chicken Broth (page 3), Vegetable Broth (page 5), or a commercial broth or bouillon cubes

1 teaspoon salt

2 tablespoons diced truffle (optional)

Heavy cream, to dribble on

Soak the porcini in about 3 cups warm water in a 2-quart bowl for 1 hour.

Melt the butter in a 4-quart heavy-bottomed pot; whisk in the flour and beat until very smooth. Whisk in the broth, sprinkle with salt, and bring to a boil. With your hands, scoop up the porcini and reserve the water for another preparation if you wish—its flavor is too strong for this soup. Add the porcini to the soup pot. Cover, reduce the heat, and simmer for 20 minutes.

For the last 5 minutes of cooking, add the optional diced truffle. Taste and correct seasoning. Serve very hot, garnished with cream.

# cauliflower soup

We generally think of nutmeg to season cauliflower, but curry is also very good—it brings out the subtle taste of cauliflower. For this soup, I season with hot curry. When you pick a cauliflower, buy a white head (the curd) without any brownish tinge—the mark of age—and old cauliflower also develops a very strong, unpleasant odor.

**For the Soup:**

1 medium cauliflower (about 2 ½ pounds)

4 tablespoons olive oil

1 large onion, peeled and chopped

2 teaspoons salt

Freshly ground black pepper

3 cups Chicken Broth (page 3), Vegetable Broth (page 5), or a commercial broth or bouillon cubes

**For the White Sauce (Béchamel):**

4 cups milk (whole, 2%, or 1%)

1 small onion, quartered

4 small bay leaves

¼ teaspoon ground mace

1 teaspoon salt

Freshly ground black pepper

2 tablespoons butter

1 tablespoon flour

1 small teaspoon curry powder

**The soup:** Discard the green leaves and hard stem of the cauliflower; break the head into flowerets, trim them, and cut off the ends; peel the tough stem skin of the older flowerets. Chop into small pieces to yield about 8 cups.

Heat the olive oil in a 6-quart heavy-bottomed pot and add the chopped onion and cauliflower. Sprinkle with salt and pepper. Cover, reduce the heat, and simmer over low heat for 15 minutes. Check once in a while to be sure neither the cauliflower nor the onion is burning.

Add the broth, bring to a boil, cover, reduce the heat, and cook at a gentle boil for 20 minutes or until the cauliflower is very tender.

**The white sauce:** Bring the milk, onion, bay leaves, mace, salt, and pepper to a boil in a 4-quart pan.

In a large heavy-bottomed saucepan, melt the butter and whisk in the flour. Add the boiling milk with the onion and bay leaves. Whisk in the curry. Reduce the heat and cook just under a boil for 30 minutes, whisking the sauce once in a while.

Discard the bay leaves. Add the white sauce to the cauliflower soup and purée the soup in a blender or food processor, or with an immersion blender.

When ready to serve, reheat the soup; taste and correct seasoning before serving.

# cauliflower soup with morels

$^1/_4$ ounce dry morels

$^1/_2$ cup water

Soak the morels in the water for $^1/_2$ hour. Strain (reserving the liquid for another preparation, like pasta) and wash them under cold running water to remove any sand clinging to the stems. Chop and poach them in the broth of the master recipe for 15 minutes. Strain the broth and follow the instructions in the Cauliflower Soup.

Reheat the morels in the soup for a garnish.

# cordon bleu jerusalem artichoke, tomato, and orange soup

Jerusalem artichokes grew wild in North and South America. Native Americans introduced them to settlers in North America; the vegetable is not from Jerusalem. In the States, they are also called sunchokes, in France, we call them *topinambours*, and I remember eating them instead of potatoes during the Second World War. Even today, there are not many French who will eat them. It's a shame; they are very good uncooked, in a salad such as Wayne Marshall's Tossed Salad (page 136). Raw, they taste like water chestnuts, and cooked, their flavor is like artichokes.

When my friend Sarah Lambert went to the Cordon Bleu in London years ago, she learned to make this soup. When I started working on this book, Sarah went back to her cooking school notebook and found this recipe. It is interesting to see how different this soup is from the French version of a Jerusalem artichoke soup (see page 28).

1 pound Jerusalem artichokes

1 tablespoon lemon juice

2 tablespoons butter

1 large onion, finely chopped (1½ cups)

2 teaspoons salt

1 (14-ounce) can plum tomatoes, drained and coarsely chopped

1 garlic clove, crushed with a little salt

3 cups Chicken Broth (page 3), Vegetable Broth (page 5), or a commercial broth or bouillon cubes

1 orange

1 bay leaf

Freshly ground black pepper

Brush the artichokes under running barely warm water; peel and drop them into a large bowl of water with the lemon juice to keep them from darkening too much while you peel them. Peel, drain, and cut the artichokes into thin slices; you should have 2½ to 3 cups.

In a 4-quart heavy-bottomed pot, melt the butter over medium heat. When the butter sizzles, add the artichokes and onion. Sprinkle with 1 teaspoon of the salt. Cover, reduce heat, and braise slowly for 10 minutes without coloring the vegetables. Add the tomatoes, garlic, and broth.

Peel the orange with a vegetable peeler and reserve the peeled orange for later. Tie the orange peel with the bay leaf and bury the packet in the soup. Sprinkle with the remaining 2 teaspoons salt and some pepper. Bring the soup to a boil. Cover, reduce the heat, and simmer gently for 35 minutes or until the artichokes are very tender.

Discard the bay leaf. Ladle by ladle, purée the soup until very smooth in a blender or food processor. Squeeze the orange for $^1/_2$ cup juice and add the juice to the soup and reheat.

Taste and correct seasoning before serving very hot.

# jerusalem artichoke soup with toasted hazelnuts

During World War II, my mother sometimes was given butter and milk from friends who came to visit us from outside Paris. She would then make soups with a béchamel (white sauce); that's when I ate my soup without too much coaxing. See the headnote of the Cordon Bleu Jerusalem Artichoke, Tomato, and Orange Soup (pages 26–27) for general information on Jerusalem artichokes.

2 pounds Jerusalem artichokes

1 tablespoon lemon juice

3 tablespoons vegetable oil

2 medium onions, peeled and thinly sliced (2 cups)

Salt

Freshly ground black pepper

3 tablespoons butter

3 tablespoons all-purpose flour

3 cups hot milk (whole, 2%, or 1%), scalded

3 cups Chicken Broth (page 3), Vegetable Broth (page 5), or a commercial broth or bouillon cubes

1/2 cup toasted hazelnuts, peeled and chopped, for garnish

Brush the artichokes under running warm water. Set in a large bowl of water with the lemon juice while you clean all the artichokes. Drain and cut them into thin slices (about 6 cups).

Heat the oil in a 6-quart heavy-bottomed pot. Add the onions and stir for 1 minute in the hot oil; cover, reduce the heat, and braise for 10 minutes without burning. Stir in the artichokes; sprinkle with salt and pepper. Cover and braise for 15 more minutes.

Meanwhile, prepare the béchamel. Melt the butter in a large heavy-bottomed saucepan, add the flour, and whisk for several seconds. Whisk in the hot milk and simmer for 5 minutes, whisking occasionally. Pour the béchamel and the broth into the soup pot and bring to a boil. Cover, reduce the heat, and cook at a gentle boil for 30 minutes or until the artichokes are tender.

In batches, purée the soup in a blender or food processor or use an immersion blender. Refrigerate until ready to eat. Reheat the soup just before serving. Taste and correct seasoning. Ladle the hot soup into individual soup bowls and garnish with toasted hazelnuts.

# chestnut soup

When I prepare a venison dinner party in the fall, I make this soup to open the festivities. It is not necessary to cook and peel chestnuts for the soup, but if you want to use fresh chestnuts, see Colette Valentin's Chestnut Salad (page 137); the water-packed chestnuts in cans are very good for soups, especially the Faugier brand.

2 tablespoons olive oil

2 medium onions, thinly sliced (2 cups)

1 (20-ounce) can whole water-packed chestnuts

5 cups Chicken Broth (page 3),
or a commercial broth or bouillon cubes

1 teaspoon salt or more

Heavy cream

Croutons (page 161)

Heat the olive oil in a 6-quart heavy-bottomed pot over moderate heat. Add the onions and cover tightly. Braise over low heat for 20 minutes or until the onions are very soft but not brown. (If necessary, add 2 to 3 tablespoons water to prevent the onions from burning.)

Drain the chestnuts and discard the liquid. Stir the chestnuts into the onions and braise for another 10 minutes.

Pour in the broth and sprinkle with salt. Bring to a boil, reduce the heat, and cook at a gentle boil, partially covered, for 30 minutes. The soup can be prepared up to this stage. Refrigerate.

One hour before eating, bring the soup back to room temperature. Just before dinnertime, purée the soup in a blender or food processor in several batches until very smooth. (I do not purée the soup ahead of time because the soup will thicken too much while waiting.) Reheat the soup, taste, and correct seasoning. To serve, dribble cream on top of each portion and serve with croutons.

# cream of celery soup

At the market in Nyons where we live for much of the year, one cold Thursday morning my husband saw and bought a beautiful bunch of celery, and he decided to come running home to make celery soup. He followed an old recipe of mine, adding cumin to the soup; the end result was a lovely lunch followed by a salad of Monkfish and Exotic Mushrooms on Mesclun (page 147).

1 bunch of celery (1 1/2 pounds)

1 medium Russet potato

1 medium onion

5 tablespoons olive oil

1 teaspoon salt

Freshly ground black pepper

1/4 teaspoon ground cumin

4 1/2 cups Chicken Broth (page 3), Vegetable Broth (page 5), or a commercial broth or bouillon cubes

1/2 cup heavy cream or half-and-half

Croutons (page 161)

Cut off the base of the celery and separate the stalks. Wash them under cold running water. Cut the stalks into 1-inch-thick slices and cut the celery leaves for 1/2 cup of chopped leaves. Peel and dice the onion and the potato.

In a 6-quart heavy-bottomed pot, heat the oil. Stir in the celery, potato, and onion. Season with salt, pepper, and cumin. Cover, reduce the heat, and braise the vegetables for 10 minutes, stirring once in a while to prevent the vegetables from burning. Add the broth and bring to a boil; cover, reduce the heat, and simmer gently for 40 minutes.

Purée the soup in a blender or food processor, or use an immersion blender. Add the cream. Just before serving, reheat the soup and add more broth if necessary. Taste and correct seasoning. Serve with croutons.

# swiss chard, potato, and carrot soup

This is the same type of soup as The "Day After" Soup (page 13) or the Monaco Spinach and Pasta Soup (page 47). It's cooked in water and takes no time to make. I love Swiss chard as much as I do spinach; if you can't find it, substitute spinach.

You can use the Swiss chard leaves and ribs for separate cooking preparations. For this soup, the leaves are cooked, but reserve the ribs and either make Spanish Chickpea and Pork Soup (page 122) or cut the ribs into 2-inch pieces and cook them for 10 minutes in broth, then drain (reserving the broth) and serve as a side dish.

1 ½ pounds Swiss chard

2 medium Russet potatoes, peeled and cut into ½-inch cubes (2 cups)

2 carrots, sliced (1 cup)

Salt

6 cups water

2 teaspoons butter or more

Chop the Swiss chard leaves; you should have 8 loosely packed cups. Place all vegetables in a 6-quart heavy-bottomed pot and sprinkle with salt. Add the water and bring to a boil. Cover, reduce the heat, and simmer for 20 minutes or until the potatoes are tender.

Purée the soup with an immersion blender, in a food mill, or very quickly in a blender or food processor in several batches. Reheat the soup; taste and correct seasoning before serving with a small pat of butter in each soup bowl.

# SQUASH
# soups

In the following three winter-squash soups, the squash is cooked by two different methods: in the Pumpkin Soup, the squash is first roasted then braised, whereas in the Butternut Soup with Cumin, the squash is braised. When I buy a butternut or banana squash, I usually have enough to make several soups. I wrap the unused portion and refrigerate it until I'm inspired to make another soup; it keeps for days.

To prepare squash, first split the vegetable in half with a large butcher's knife. Scoop out the seeds and stringy parts attached to the flesh; don't worry if there are bits of string left. Cut each half in slices, then cut each slice into several pieces. Holding each piece, slice off the peel with a butcher's knife. Slice off any remaining strings.

# butternut soup with cumin

For this soup, cook your favorite winter squash.

3 tablespoons olive oil

3 medium onions, peeled and sliced (3 cups)

3 pounds butternut squash,
peeled and cut into 2-inch cubes (8 cups)

2 teaspoons salt

Freshly ground black pepper

1 teaspoon ground cumin

3 sprigs of fresh thyme

3 cups Chicken Broth (page 3),
Vegetable Broth (page 5), or a commercial broth
or bouillon cubes

Croutons (page 161)

In a 6-quart heavy-bottomed soup pot, heat the oil over medium heat and stir in the onions. Cover, reduce the heat, and braise for 15 minutes, checking that the onions don't burn.

Add the squash to the onions. Sprinkle with salt, pepper, cumin, and thyme; cover the pot. Braise for another 15 minutes, checking once in a while that the vegetables do not burn.

Add the broth, bring to a boil, cover, reduce the heat, and simmer for 30 minutes or until the squash is tender.

Purée the soup in a blender or food processor in batches or use an immersion blender. Reheat the soup; taste for salt, and add more cumin to taste. Serve boiling hot with croutons.

# pumpkin soup

Sarah Lambert, my cooking and swimming partner, is a superb professional cook. She studied cooking at the English Cordon Bleu, then went on to be chef at Banners, a restaurant in Winchester, Hampshire, England. She roasts slices of pumpkin or butternut squash in the oven first, then braises them with onions in chicken broth. To serve, she puts a bit of fontina cheese in the bottom of each bowl and pours the hot soup over it. Marc Meneau from L'Esperance, a very nice restaurant in Burgundy, tops his pumpkin soup with bread crumbs and cheese and puts it under the broiler, just like an onion soup. Both methods are delicious and very filling. I follow with a salad like the one I make with *haricots verts* (see page 141).

4 pounds pumpkin or squash, not peeled

5 tablespoons olive oil

2 medium onions, sliced (2 cups)

2 teaspoons salt

Freshly ground black pepper

1/8 teaspoon grated nutmeg

5 cups Chicken Broth (page 3), Vegetable Broth (page 5), or commercial broth or bouillon cubes

4 ounces fontina cheese, diced

Preheat the oven to 425 degrees.

Cut the pumpkin or butternut squash into 2-inch slices. Do not peel, but scoop out the seeds and cut off the stringy mush. Brush 2 tablespoons olive oil over the slices and place on a cookie sheet lined with aluminum foil, peel against the paper. Roast for 30 minutes.

When squash is cool enough to handle, slice off the peel with a large chef's knife. If any of the flesh has burned, cut that off, too. Cut the roasted pumpkin into 2-inch cubes (about 6 cups).

Heat the remaining 3 tablespoons olive oil in a 6-quart heavy-bottomed soup pot and add the onions. Cover, reduce the heat, and braise the onions for 5 minutes without coloring. Stir in the squash and sprinkle with salt, pepper, and nutmeg. Cover and braise for another 5 minutes. Pour in the broth, bring to a boil, cover, reduce the heat, and simmer for 20 minutes or until the squash is very tender.

Purée the soup in a blender or food processor, ladle by ladle, or use an immersion blender.

Reheat the soup; while it's reheating, sprinkle the cheese in the bottom of the soup bowls. Taste and correct seasoning before pouring the hot soup over the cheese.

VARIATION:

# mark meneau's pumpkin soup gratin

**For Each Soup Bowl:**

$1/3$ cup grated Gruyère or Appenzeller cheese

$1/3$ cup bread crumbs

Olive oil, to drizzle

Turn the broiler to high.

Pour the hot soup into individual ovenproof bowls. Mix the cheese and the bread crumbs and sprinkle it on top of the soup. Drizzle olive oil over the cheese and bread crumbs. Put the bowls on a cookie sheet and place them in the broiler below the heating element. Broil for just a minute or until the top of the soups are golden brown.

# celery root and potato soup with braised shallots

When I started teaching cooking in New York in the early seventies, it was almost impossible to find celery root, also called celeriac or celery knob. Today, most of the greengrocers and upscale supermarkets sell it in the fall and winter. If you have never bought a celeriac, don't be put off by its appearance; it is not appetizing, even down-right ugly, but persevere—you will be surprised by the delicate flavor of this vegetable. Scrub it under running cold water, then with a large knife, quarter it before peeling it. To peel, slice off the peel as you would a pumpkin (see page 32). Just like a pumpkin or winter squash, you lose a lot of volume; a 2-pound celeriac peeled will weigh approximately 1 1/2 pounds.

1 1/4-pound celery root,
peeled and cut into 1/2-inch cubes (3 cups)

1 large Russet potato,
peeled and quartered (1 cup)

2 leeks, white part and light green leaves,
chopped (2 cups)

3 quarts Chicken Broth (page 3),
Vegetable Broth (page 5), or a commercial broth
or bouillon cubes

1 tablespoon salt

3 tablespoons butter

5 large shallots, peeled and minced (1 cup)

Freshly ground black pepper

1/2 cup minced chives

Potato Puffs (page 37)

Put the celery root, potato, leeks, broth, and a sprinkling of salt in a 9-quart, heavy-bottomed pot. Bring to a boil, cover, reduce the heat, and cook at a gentle boil for 30 minutes or until the celery is very tender. Cool for 15 minutes.

In several batches, purée the soup in a blender or food processor very quickly to avoid making the potato gummy, or use an immersion blender.

In a large skillet, melt the butter. Stir in the shallots, cover the skillet, and reduce the heat. Braise for 5 to 7 minutes or until the shallots wilt but do not burn. Check occasionally.

Stir the shallots into the soup. Taste and correct the seasoning, adding pepper. Just before serving, reheat the soup and add more broth if necessary. Garnish with minced chives and serve potato puffs on the side.

# potato puffs

These little potato puffs are great with vegetable soups.

1 pound Russet potatoes, peeled and quartered

Salt

¹/₂ cup all-purpose flour

1 quart corn oil, for frying

In a medium saucepan, cover the potatoes with water, add salt, and bring to a boil over moderate heat. Cook until the potatoes are very tender, 20 to 30 minutes. Drain well.

Quickly pass the potatoes through a ricer or beat in the bowl of a heavy-duty standing mixer with the paddle attachment while they are still hot.

In a large bowl, combine the potatoes and flour; stir until smooth. On a floured board and with a floured rolling pin, gently roll out the dough to a 12-inch round. Stamp out 2 ¹/₂-inch rounds with the floured rim of a glass or a cookie cutter. Roll out the scraps and stamp out more rounds. Place the rounds on a clean kitchen towel.

In a large, deep skillet, heat the oil to 325 degrees. Add the potato rounds in three batches and fry until puffed and golden brown. Transfer the puffs to a serving platter lined with a clean kitchen towel. Sprinkle with salt and serve right away.

# celery root soup with stilton

Celery root is one of my favorite root vegetables. I make soups, gratins, and chips with it during the winter. This recipe comes from England and is served with crumbled Stilton. Blue cheese or Roquefort is also very good with it.

2 tablespoons butter

1 tablespoon oil

2 medium onions, peeled and chopped (2 cups)

1 large carrot, peeled and chopped ($^1/_2$ cup)

Sea salt

1 $^1/_2$-pound celery root, peeled and cut into 1-inch cubes (about 4 cups)

Freshly ground black pepper

8 cups Chicken Broth (page 3), Vegetable Broth (page 5), or a commercial broth or bouillon cubes

4 sprigs of fresh thyme

1 $^1/_2$ cups milk (whole, 2%, or 1%)

Several sprigs of fresh parsley, finely chopped

4 ounces Stilton, blue cheese, or Roquefort

Poilane's Rye and Nut Bread (page 157)

Heat the butter and oil in a 6-quart heavy-bottomed pot. Stir in the onions and carrot. Sprinkle with 1 teaspoon salt. Cover, reduce the heat, and braise slowly for 10 minutes, stirring the onions from time to time to make sure they do not burn.

Add the celery root to the onion-carrot mixture, sprinkle salt and pepper over the vegetables. Pour in the broth, add the thyme, and bring to a boil; cover, reduce the heat, and cook at a gentle boil for 1 hour or until the vegetables are tender.

When the soup is cool, purée in batches in a blender or food processor, or use an immersion blender.

Reheat the soup with the milk and more broth if it is too thick. Taste and correct the seasoning with more salt and pepper if necessary. Fold in the chopped parsley. Bring back to a boil. Serve with crumbled cheese over each portion of soup and bread slices on the side.

# brunoise soup

A brunoise soup is made by stewing aromatic vegetables such as carrots, leeks or onions, turnips, and celeriac in butter before adding water or broth. The vegetables must be diced very fine (1/8 inch and I am not kidding), which is a time-consuming affair, but it does not taste as good when I cheat. Otherwise, the soup is simplicity itself. For a dinner party, you could serve just the brunoise stewed in butter and pour in clarified broth (page 7) for a *consomme à la brunoise.*

5 tablespoons butter

3 cups finely diced carrots

1 1/2 cups finely diced turnip

1 cup finely diced celeriac

1 cup finely diced leeks or onions

10 cups water, Vegetable Broth (page 5), or a commercial broth

1 tablespoon salt

Freshly ground black pepper

In a 6-quart heavy-bottomed pot, melt the butter over low heat. Add all the vegetables and stir. Cover very tightly and braise for 20 minutes without coloring the vegetables, checking occasionally. Let the water gathered on the underside of the lid fall back into the vegetables when opening the pot. Your kitchen will smell heavenly.

Add the water or broth. Sprinkle with the salt and pepper. Raise the heat and bring to a boil. Cover, reduce the heat, and cook at a gentle boil for 1 hour.

Strain the vegetables in a fine-meshed strainer clamped onto a large mixing bowl. There should be 5 cups of liquid; if there is more, boil it down.

Reheat the broth and vegetables. Taste and correct seasoning. Serve very hot.

# jamaican kale and scotch bonnet pepper soup

In the original Jamaican recipe, the broth is made with a pig's tail and with salt beef. In the States, I boil down beef broth to substitute for the pig's tail and salt beef. The combination of rich broth and coconut milk is delicious.

6 cups Beef Broth (page 2),
or a commercial broth or bouillon cubes

1 cup canned coconut milk

4 cups chopped raw kale (1/2 pound)

1 Scotch bonnet chile

1 scallion, trimmed and sliced

1 sweet potato (1/3 pound), diced

Salt

In a 4-quart heavy-bottomed pot, boil down the broth to 4 cups to concentrate its flavor. Add the coconut milk, kale, chile, scallion, and sweet potato. Bring to a boil, reduce the heat, and cook at a gentle boil, partially covered, for 1 hour.

Discard the chile, then taste and correct the seasoning with salt if necessary.

# yellow turnip and onion soup

Yellow turnips or rutabagas are a big mystery to me. They are found in all kinds of vegetable markets and supermarkets, but I never see anybody buy them or cook with them. I know why the French are not very fond of them; during World War II, rutabagas and Jerusalem artichokes were about the only vegetables available.

Rutabagas are not overly loved in the States either, and it's a pity—they are a wonderful vegetable. The yellow turnips are generally waxed to prevent dehydration, making them difficult to peel. You need to use a large chef's knife and slice off layers of wax and thick peels as for winter squash and celeriac. If you persist, you will enjoy one of my favorite soups. My sister-in-law, who really believes I am the cat's meow in cooking, was taken aback when I cooked this soup; do not be put off by the strong flavor at first while it cooks; it gradually mellows to a sweet aroma in contact with the onions.

1 yellow turnip (about 3 pounds)

1 1/2 pounds onions

4 tablespoons butter or olive oil

1 tablespoon salt

Freshly ground black pepper

2 1/2 quarts Chicken Broth (page 3), Vegetable Broth (page 5), or a commercial broth or bouillon cubes

Slice off thick peels of the yellow turnip, and using the point of the knife, break into chunks. Cut the chunks into 1/2-inch cubes (8 cups). Peel and chop the onions (1 1/2 cups).

In a 9-quart heavy-bottomed pot, melt the butter over medium heat. Add the turnips and onions. Season with salt and pepper. Cover, reduce the heat, and braise for 45 minutes, stirring once in a while.

Add the broth, bring to a boil, cover, reduce the heat, and cook at a gentle boil for 1/2 hour or until the turnip is very soft.

Purée with an immersion blender, or in a blender or food processor in several batches.

Reheat the soup; taste and correct seasoning before serving.

# 42 spring

When spring arrives, the long dark days of winter are gone and our weekly food market in Nyons seems to get larger: more vendors with happy faces, selling their first asparagus, lovely fresh watercress, tender spinach leaves, and strawberries. This is the time when I see young white turnips (and again in the fall) and brilliant green peas—I could eat fresh peas every day during that period. I also love fava beans; when they are just very young, they can be eaten raw. And we know summer will bring more and more vegetables for ratatouille, etc. It seems a rebirth of nature in the stalls of our market! Most of these soups in this chapter are great starters for dinner parties.

# asparagus soup

I serve this soup as soon as asparagus is in my weekly farmer's market. If you are not cooking the asparagus right away, refrigerate it wrapped in a wet cloth; it will keep for a few days.

2 pounds asparagus

8 cups Chicken Broth (page 3),
Vegetable Broth (page 5), or a commercial broth
or bouillon cubes

1 teaspoon sugar

$1/2$ teaspoon salt

Heavy cream, for garnish (optional)

Cut off about $1/2$ inch of the tough ends if necessary, then with a vegetable peeler, peel the spears up to the tips. Slice the asparagus spears into 1-inch pieces (about 6 cups) and reserve the tips for later.

Bring 6 cups of broth to a boil in a 6-quart heavy-bottomed pot. Add the asparagus pieces and sprinkle with sugar and salt. Cover and reduce the heat. Cook with the liquid bubbling gently for 20 minutes or until the asparagus is very tender (I test the doneness with a knife). Cool.

Purée the soup in several batches in a blender or food processor. Sometimes, there are asparagus fibers that do not purée in the soup (especially if the stems of the asparagus have not been peeled enough); if so, pass the soup through a sieve to discard the fibers. Reserve.

Bring 2 cups of broth to a boil, add the asparagus tips, and cook until just tender, about 5 minutes. Scoop out the tips and transfer them to the soup pot. Reserve the broth.

When ready to serve, reheat the soup and add enough more broth to thin out the soup, which will have thickened while waiting. (What's left of the broth, keep for another soup.) Taste and adjust seasoning. Dribble cream over the soup if you wish.

# spinach and watercress soup

I am proud of this soup: it's beautiful to look at and it's delicious. I make it with fresh spinach that I buy in bulk at the market. It's true that I abhor cleaning the spinach leaves, especially when they are full of sand, but what a reward afterward!

1 small celery root (about 1/2 pound), peeled

1 leek

4 large shallots, peeled

2 tablespoons olive oil

2 teaspoons salt

2 pounds loose spinach leaves or 3 (10-ounce) bags fresh spinach

1/2 pound watercress (1 bunch)

5 cups Chicken Broth (page 3), Vegetable Broth (page 5), or a commercial broth or bouillon cubes

Heavy cream, for the garnish (optional)

Cut the celery root into 1/4-inch cubes (about 2 cups). Slit the leek lengthwise up to 1/2 inch of the stem and wash under cold water. Cut off all the dark green leaves and reserve for a broth. Cut the white of the leek into 1/4-inch slices (about 1 1/2 cups). Coarsely chop the shallots (about 1/2 cup). You should have about 4 cups total of celery root, leek, and shallots.

Heat the oil in a 6-quart heavy-bottomed pot over moderate heat. Add the celery root, leek, and shallots. Sprinkle with 1 teaspoon salt, cover, and braise for 15 minutes without coloring, checking once in a while. Add 1/4 cup water to the pot if the vegetables start to color.

To clean the spinach, place it in the sink filled with lukewarm water (cold water numbs your fingers) and remove the stems by folding each spinach leaf in one hand and tearing off the stem with the other hand.

Discard the stems. Soak the spinach in lots of water several times in the sink; the sand will go to the bottom of the sink. In batches, stack a large handful of leaves and chop coarsely.

Rinse the watercress and coarsely chop the leaves and stems. Add the spinach to the vegetables in the pot, cover, and braise for 10 minutes until the spinach is totally wilted.

Pour the broth over the vegetables and bring to a rolling boil. Add the watercress. Bring to a boil again and sprinkle with remaining 1 teaspoon salt. As soon as the soup is boiling, turn off the heat and let cool.

Ladle by ladle, purée the soup in a blender or food processor. Reheat when ready to serve. Taste and correct seasoning. Serve very hot. Decorate the soup, if you wish, with drizzles of heavy cream.

# belgian watercress and leek soup

Arlette Brisson, a long-time New Yorker, makes this wonderful Belgian soup from her native country with local watercress and leeks. She boils watercress with the stems for less than a minute to retain the brilliant emerald color. The soup looks so appetizing that you almost forget how good it tastes. Both Arlette's watercress soup and the recipe that precedes it, Spinach and Watercress Soup (page 44), are excellent cold as well as hot!

1 ½ pounds watercress with stems
(about 3 bunches)

4 large leeks, white part only,
washed and sliced (6 cups)

1 large Yukon Gold potato,
peeled and cut into 1-inch cubes (1 ½ cups)

4 cups Chicken Broth (page 3),
Vegetable Broth (page 5), or a commercial broth
or bouillon cubes

2 teaspoons salt

In a 6-quart heavy-bottomed pot, bring a large amount of water to a hard boil. Add the watercress, bring back to a boil, sprinkle with 1 teaspoon salt, and count just under 1 minute boiling all the while. Immediately drain the watercress in a colander, reserving 1 cup of the liquid. Rinse the watercress under running cold water for 1 minute.

Purée the watercress with the reserved cooking water in a food processor until very smooth. Reserve.

Combine the leeks and potato in the same pot. Add 3 cups broth and 1 teaspoon salt. Bring to a boil, cover, reduce the heat, and cook with the liquid bubbling gently for 20 minutes.

In small batches (about ½ cup at a time), purée the soup in a blender for only 3 seconds to avoid creating gummy potatoes. Combine the leek and potato soup with the purée of the watercress in the soup pot. Taste and correct seasoning with remaining salt. Add more broth to the soup if you find it too thick and reheat just before serving time. Serve very hot.

# monaco spinach and pasta soup

I was intrigued with this recipe, which I found in a cookbook on Monaco. This is how it read: "For 3 ½ soup plates filled with liquid serving 2 eaters." I went to the kitchen to check on the volume of one French soup plate (about 1 cup), I also presumed that I needed 3½ soup plates of liquid for two plates of finished soup because of evaporation while the soup cooks. I decided to try the recipe; it was a cinch to make and good to eat.

I use a thin pasta that cooks quickly. The soup takes 15 minutes to prepare and less than 10 minutes to cook.

1 pound loose spinach
or 1 (10-ounce) bag fresh spinach

2 eggs

½ cup grated Gruyère cheese

Freshly grated nutmeg

1 teaspoon salt

Freshly ground black pepper

3 cups Chicken Broth (page 3),
Vegetable Broth (page 5), or a commercial broth
or bouillon cubes

¾ cup orzo or thin vermicelli

Wash the spinach in a sink filled with warm water. Discard the thick stems. With a large chef's knife, chop the spinach (4 cups loosely packed).

Break the eggs into a large bowl and beat them as for an omelet. Stir in the spinach and grated cheese; season with nutmeg, salt, and pepper.

In a 4-quart pan, bring the broth to a boil. Add the pasta and spinach mixture. Cover and simmer at a gentle boil for 5 minutes or until the pasta is cooked. Taste and correct seasoning with perhaps more nutmeg before serving.

# florentine tomato and spinach soup

Debbie Ahern came to cook with me last summer in Provence. I recognized a talented natural cook and was more than willing to test and taste her favorite soup. Being too modest, she remarked, "I think it's okay, but everyone I serve it to goes gaga. I really don't understand as it's the easiest thing to make." I do understand—good home-made beef or chicken broth, tomatoes, spinach, pasta, and grated cheese—the combination is magic.

2 pounds fresh tomatoes,
peeled and chopped (6 cups)

1 medium onion, sliced

1 celery stalk, diced

5 cups Beef Broth (page 2), Chicken Broth
(page 3), Vegetable Broth (page 5),
or a commercial broth or bouillon cubes

1 tablespoon fresh lemon juice

4 whole cloves

2 teaspoons salt

²/₃ cup small macaroni shells

1 pound loose spinach
or 1 (10-ounce bag) fresh spinach

2 tablespoons vegetable or olive oil

A bowl of grated Gruyère or Parmesan cheese

A loaf of bread, Poilane (page 156)
or Tuscan (page 158)

Put the tomatoes, onion, celery stalk, and broth in a 6-quart heavy-bottomed pot. Bring to a boil, cover, reduce the heat, and simmer for 20 minutes. Add the lemon juice, cloves, and salt. Simmer for another 15 minutes.

Fill a 4-quart pan with water. Bring it to a boil and add the macaroni shells. At a steady boil, cook the shells until tender. Drain and reserve.

Discard the spinach stems and wash the leaves thoroughly in a sink full of warm water. Chop the spinach coarsely.

Heat the oil in a large nonstick skillet. Add half the spinach and over high heat, stir-fry it in batches for a minute or until just wilted.

Reheat the soup with the macaroni and the spinach. Taste and correct the seasoning before serving with a bowl of grated cheese, accompanied by thick slices of bread.

# fava bean soup with mint and feta cheese

I ate this soup in London several springs ago. I loved it and was able to re-create it at home. Fava beans can be tricky. They appear in spring and as the season advances, the beans become bigger and more floury; they also lose their brilliant green color and fade to yellow. The soup is at its best when the beans are small and brilliant green. Fava beans have two layers of protection—the pod and then each bean has skin that is removed by boiling for a minute. This part is tedious, but the result makes it worth your time. Have more broth in hand to thin out the soup, prepared ahead of time.

5 pounds fresh fava beans
in their pods, shelled (5 cups)

5 tablespoons olive oil

2 medium onions, thinly sliced (2 cups)

20 leaves of fresh mint

2 teaspoons salt

5 cups Chicken Broth (page 3),
Vegetable Broth (page 5), or a commercial broth
or bouillon cubes

1/4 pound feta cheese, diced

Bring a large pot of water to a boil, add the beans, and bring back to a boil. Drain immediately and place under cold running water. Peel each bean. Cut off the top of the bean with a knife, then slip it out of the shell with your thumb and index finger (about 3 cups). This step takes about 15 minutes but the rest of the recipe is easy.

In a 6-quart heavy-bottomed pot, heat the oil over medium heat, add the onions and favas, and stir. Cover, reduce the heat, and braise for 5 minutes. Add the mint and sprinkle with salt. Pour in the broth and bring to a boil. Cover, reduce the heat, and simmer for 25 minutes.

In batches, purée the soup in a blender or food processor. To make it silky smooth, pass the soup through a strainer.

Just before serving, reheat the soup with the feta cheese and thin it with more broth as it thickens while waiting; taste and correct seasoning.

# joel robuchon's fresh pea and fava bean soup

Joel Robuchon is one of today's great French chefs. The only tedious part of this recipe is shelling the fava beans twice, first by removing them from their pods, then boiling them to remove the skin. It's easy to do but it takes a while. See the head-note for the previous recipe. It's a great soup for a dinner party; it can be made ahead of time but only make it in the spring when both garden peas and fava beans are in season.

2 pounds fava beans in their pod, shelled (2 to 3 cups)

2 tablespoons butter

1 large shallot, peeled and minced

2 pounds peas in their pod, shelled (about 2 1/2 cups)

1 1/2 teaspoons salt

Freshly ground black pepper

4 cups Chicken Broth (page 3), Vegetable Broth (page 5), or a commercial broth or bouillon cubes

Heavy cream, to drizzle

In a 6-quart heavy-bottomed pot, bring about 3 quarts of water to a boil. When boiling, add the fava beans and bring the water back to a boil. Turn off the heat and drain the beans in a large colander. Refresh under running cold water to stop the cooking. Remove the germ on top of each bean and with your thumb and index finger, push out the bean.

Once more in the soup pot, bring about 3 quarts of water to a boil. Add the favas and boil for 5 minutes. Drain in a large colander.

In the same pot, melt the butter and when it sizzles, stir in the shallot. Cover, reduce the heat, and braise for 5 minutes without coloring. Add the beans and peas to the soup pot.

Sprinkle with salt and pepper, then pour in the broth. Bring to a boil, cover, reduce the heat, and simmer at a gentle boil for 15 to 20 minutes or until the peas and beans are very tender.

Purée the soup, ladle by ladle, in a blender for a long time to make the soup very smooth. (Robuchon puts the soup through a drum sieve for a very smooth texture.)

When ready to serve, reheat the soup, taste, and correct the seasoning, adding more broth if the soup thickens, which it will do standing while waiting for dinner.

Decorate individual preheated soup plates with heavy cream.

# takishamaya pea and snow pea soup

Ellen Greaves, who was the chef at Takishamaya restaurant on Fifth Avenue in New York, and Wayne Nish, chef and owner of March, a four-star restaurant just a few blocks away, have written a lovely cookbook called *Simple Menus for the Bento Box: Seasonal American Meals and Japanese Presentations.* They created an excellent pea and snow pea soup that's a favorite at the downstairs restaurant of the Japanese store. Several years ago, they generously gave me the recipe.

1 pound snow peas

4 cups Chicken Broth, or more if necessary (page 3), or a commercial broth or bouillon cubes

2 teaspoons salt

Freshly ground black pepper

4 cups frozen small peas (petits pois)

Heavy cream

Minced chives

Cut off the tips of the snow peas and remove the strings if necessary. Cut each snow pea in half. Cover the snow peas with the broth in a 6-quart heavy-bottomed pot. Sprinkle with salt and pepper. Bring to a boil, reduce the heat, and cook at a gentle boil, partially covered, for 10 minutes or until the snow peas are tender.

Add the frozen peas and bring the soup back to a boil; reduce the heat, cover, and simmer for 5 minutes.

A little at a time, purée the peas in a blender until very smooth. Strain the soup through a sieve. Taste and correct the seasoning with salt and pepper.

Before serving, reheat the soup; if it is too thick, add more broth to thin it to the consistency you like. (This is likely necessary if the soup stands for a while before reheating.) Serve in individual hot soup bowls, dribbled with cream and garnished with chives.

# white turnip soup with morels

White turnips have two seasons: spring and early fall. They are at their best when small, with a white crispy flesh; avoid the kind we see often in supermarkets, those large round bulbs with a pithy, cardboard-like texture. Morels are picked in the spring, but for most of us, fresh morels are not usually available and the dried ones are perfectly acceptable.

4 tablespoons olive oil

1 1/2 pounds white turnips,
peeled and thinly sliced (6 cups)

2 Russet potatoes, peeled and quartered (2 cups)

1 medium onion,
peeled and coarsely chopped (1 cup)

1 1/4 teaspoons salt or more

Freshly ground black pepper

5 cups Chicken Broth (page 3),
Vegetable Broth (page 5), or a commercial broth
or bouillon cubes

1/3 cup dried morels

1 cup hot water

1 tablespoon butter

Croutons (page 161)

In a 6-quart heavy-bottomed pot, heat the oil over medium heat. Sauté the turnips, potatoes, and onion in the oil for 5 minutes, or until golden, stirring occasionally. Sprinkle with 1 teaspoon salt and some pepper. Cover, reduce the heat, and braise for 20 minutes.

Add the broth and bring to a boil. Cover, reduce the heat, and simmer for 30 minutes or until the vegetables are tender.

Meanwhile, soak the morels in the hot water for 30 minutes. Drain the morels in a cheesecloth-lined strainer; reserve the liquid. Wash the morels once more under running cold water to discard the remaining sand clinging to their stems. Chop the morels coarsely.

In a 2-quart saucepan, boil down the morel juice to about 1/4 cup. Add the morels and butter, and sprinkle with remaining salt. Cover the pan, reduce the heat, and braise the morels for 5 minutes. Turn off the heat and set aside.

Purée the soup with an immersion blender or 1/2 cup at a time, very quickly (so the potatoes don't get gummy), in a blender or food processor.

Just before serving, reheat the soup with the morels; taste and correct the seasoning before serving the soup. Serve croutons on the side.

# richard olney's artichoke soup

In the late sixties and early seventies, I read and cooked every recipe that Richard Olney wrote for *Cuisine et Vins de France,* a French culinary magazine. I had learned to cook from watching my mother, then my aunt in the kitchen, but it is by reading Olney that I became a cook. I fell in love with every word he wrote and followed religiously what he said. The results were always excellent. The magazine articles became his first cookbook, the classic *French Menu Cookbook.*

This soup is adapted from that book. Richard recommended to scrape the meat off each artichoke leaf, a tedious business if you are alone doing the work. I serve the leaves as an appetizer with an oil and vinegar dressing; that way everybody dips the leaves in the dressing and enjoys the meat of the artichoke leaves. He decorated the soup with chopped toasted hazelnuts, but I prefer croutons.

8 large artichokes

1 lemon

6 cups Chicken Broth (page 3),
or a commercial broth or bouillon cubes

3 tablespoons butter

3 tablespoons all-purpose flour

Salt

Croutons (page 161)

Snap off the long stem at the base of each artichoke. Slice off the top of the leaves with a serrated knife and rub lemon juice over the exposed leaves. In a 15-quart stockpot, bring a large amount of salted water to a boil, add the artichokes, and cook for 30 minutes until very tender. Drain the artichokes in a large colander and cool.

Heat the broth in a 4-quart saucepan.

In a 6-quart pot, melt the butter over moderate heat; whisk the flour into the melted butter until smooth, then whisk in the hot broth and add salt. Cover, reduce the heat, and simmer for 30 minutes, whisking the mixture once in a while.

Meanwhile, pull off all the leaves of the artichokes and save them for a snack, dunking them in a vinaigrette dressing (page 135) and biting off just the tender part of each leaf. With the point of a small knife, cut out the hairy choke from each artichoke heart. Quarter the artichoke hearts.

In a blender or food processor, purée the artichoke hearts with 2 cups of the soup. Whisk this artichoke purée into the soup.

Just before serving, reheat the soup and add more broth if the soup is too thick; taste and correct the seasoning. Serve hot with croutons.

# summer

I never had a garden until now, having lived in big cities, but it was worth waiting for. My garden is a small jewel, a suspended area of several terraces (like Nebuchadnezzar's Babylonian garden on a modest scale) carved in a hill in the center of Nyons. With it comes a large terrace shaded by a vine of Muscat grapes under which we have lunches and dinners during the summer. For luncheons, I like to serve cold soups; and for dinners, I sometimes serve warm or hot summer soups. My repertoire is a small one, but each soup in it is delicious. Some soups are more work than others, but they all are made ahead of time, which gives me the opportunity to enjoy lunch or dinner with my guests. For those soups, I prefer plates to bowls for the visual aspect (there is more surface to look at). Also, for cold soups, I stack the plates in the refrigerator and they do take less space than bowls. I keep them there at least two hours or one hour in the freezer.

# susan friedland's borscht

Friend and editor Susan Friedland serves this classic cold borscht on her New York terrace. This soup is easy to make; the one that follows is a creation of three cooks including myself and is much more work.

2 pounds beets (8 to 10 medium), washed and trimmed

Salt

1 tablespoon lemon juice

Sugar

2 boiled potatoes, peeled and halved (optional)

2 hard-boiled eggs, chopped (optional)

2 scallions, trimmed and chopped (optional)

1 cucumber, peeled and chopped (optional)

Bowl of sour cream

Cover the beets with lightly salted water in a 6-quart pot and bring to a boil. Reduce the heat and cook at a gentle boil, partially covered, for 1 hour or until the beets are tender. Drain the beets in a sieve clamped above a large bowl. Reserve the liquid. Let cool before peeling the beets. (To peel the beets, I put on thin plastic surgical gloves to keep my hands from getting stained.) Trim away any pieces of root and stem remaining. Dice, grate, or julienne the beets and place them in a tureen. Pour the beat liquid over them and refrigerate.

Just before serving, add the lemon juice and sugar to taste. (Sugar is classic in a borscht, but don't bother if you don't find it necessary.)

Garnish the soup with potato, chopped egg, scallions, or cucumber, if desired. Serve the borscht chilled with a bowl of sour cream nearby.

# my version of borscht

This take on borscht is a creation of two friends and myself. It's a beautiful soup to serve guests on a very hot day. Refrigerate the soup plates for several hours; the soup must be ice cold.

1 pound beets

2 tablespoons butter

2 medium onions, peeled and coarsely chopped (about 2 cups)

2 large garlic cloves, peeled and coarsely chopped (about 1 tablespoon)

$1/2$ cup finely diced celery

$1 1/2$ pounds tomatoes, peeled, seeded, and chopped (about 2 cups)

8 cups Beef Broth (page 2), or a commercial broth or bouillon cubes

1 tablespoon white wine vinegar or more to taste

1 tablespoon sugar

2 teaspoons–1 tablespoon salt

Freshly ground black pepper

Bowl of sour cream

Cover the beets with a large amount of water in a 9-quart heavy-bottomed pot. Bring to a boil, cover, reduce the heat, and simmer for 1 hour or until very tender. Drain the beets and refresh under running cold water. Peel the beets. (I put on thin plastic surgical gloves to keep my hands from getting stained.) Cut the beets into $1/2$-inch cubes and reserve.

Melt the butter in the same pot and stir in the onions, garlic, celery, and tomatoes. Cover and braise for 10 minutes over low to medium heat. Add the beets, broth, vinegar, and sugar to the pot. Season with salt and pepper. Bring to a boil, cover, reduce the heat, and simmer for 30 minutes. Cool the soup before the next step.

In several batches, purée the soup in a blender. Remember to fill the blender bowl only half full to prevent the soup from spurting all over the counter and kitchen walls. Taste and adjust seasoning with salt, pepper, and perhaps more vinegar. Cool the soup and refrigerate it until ready to serve.

Serve the borscht in chilled soup plates with a bowl of sour cream nearby.

# cold cucumber soup

Choose seedless cucumbers if at all possible. This soup is just an appetizer, a teaser to open up the appetite.

3 pounds cucumbers, peeled

Sea salt

1 cup plain yogurt

1 cup half-and-half

1 tablespoon lemon juice or more

1 large sprig of fresh mint

4–6 leaves of mint, for the garnish

If the cucumbers have seeds, split them in half lengthwise, and with a grapefruit spoon, scoop out the seeds and discard. Slice the cucumbers into paper-thin slices. Put them in a colander set in the sink or over a large bowl. Sprinkle about 2 teaspoons of salt over the cucumber slices and let stand for 1 hour to disgorge their water.

Wash the cucumbers under running cold water to wash off the salt. Let drain 5 minutes, then with your hands, squeeze out as much moisture as possible. Purée the cucumbers in the food processor in two batches yielding 3 cups.

Pour the cucumber purée into a small serving bowl or tureen and whisk in the yogurt, half-and-half, and lemon juice. Taste and adjust the seasonings to your taste. Bury the mint in the soup and refrigerate for several hours or overnight.

Just before serving, discard the sprig of mint. Decorate the soup with mint leaves.

# guatemalan avocado soup

What a treat on a hot day to prepare a dish with no cooking, but the success of this soup depends on the avocados. Hass avocados are considered the best; buy avocados that are firm to the touch without any brown spots and let them finish ripening in your kitchen in a paper bag with an apple. As soon as they yield to gentle pressure, they are ready. Do not forget the garnish of chopped cilantro; it really adds to the taste of the soup.

5 ripe Hass avocados, peeled and cut into slices

4 cups or more Chicken Broth (page 3), Vegetable Broth (page 5), or a commercial broth or bouillon cubes

Juice of 1 lime

1/4 cup heavy cream

1 tablespoon salt

Freshly ground black pepper

1/2 cup loosely packed minced cilantro leaves

In several batches, purée the avocados with the broth, lime juice, and cream in a blender. If you find the soup too thick, add more broth.

Add the salt gradually, tasting as you go along. Sprinkle with pepper. Refrigerate several hours.

When ready to eat the soup, chop the cilantro and sprinkle on top of the individual portions.

# carrot soup with hot curry

I like this soup so much that during the summer I serve it cold, and for the Thanksgiving and Christmas holidays I serve it hot.

4 tablespoons (1/4 cup) butter

1 medium onion, peeled and sliced (1 cup)

3 cups sliced carrots

2 teaspoons salt

Freshly ground black pepper

1/2 teaspoon hot curry powder or more to taste

1 strip of lemon peel

5 cups Chicken Broth (page 3),
or a commercial broth or bouillon cubes

1 cup cream or half-and-half

Chopped scallions (optional)

Melt the butter in a 4-quart heavy-bottomed pot; add the onion and carrots, cover, and braise for 10 minutes, stirring once in a while. Add 1/2 teaspoon salt, some pepper, the curry powder, and the lemon peel. Continue braising for another 5 minutes. Pour in the broth and sprinkle with the remaining salt. Bring to a boil; cover and simmer for 40 minutes or until the carrots are tender. Remove from the heat and let cool for 10 minutes.

Purée the soup in a blender or the food processor in several batches. Add the cream. Taste and correct seasoning.

Serve chilled in the summer or reheat the soup in winter. Decorate with chopped scallions if you wish.

# cold summer squash soup

Make this soup in late summer when gardens are overrun with squash. The taste is subtle, and for this reason it should be salted correctly: the soup will taste bland if there is not enough salt to bring out the flavor of the squash. Add more nutmeg to the soup if you do not want to add more salt.

2 tablespoons vegetable oil

1 small onion, sliced ($1/2$ cup)

4 pounds zucchini, peeled, seeded, and sliced (10 cups)

1 tablespoon salt or more

Large pinch of nutmeg

Freshly ground black pepper

1 large bay leaf

1 chicken bouillon cube dissolved in 1 cup water

2 cups milk (whole, 2%, or 1%)

$1/4$ cup fine semolina

$1/4$ cup heavy cream

1 $1/2$ tablespoons butter

Minced dill, for garnish

In a 9-quart heavy-bottomed pot, heat the oil and stir in the onion. Cook over medium-high heat until wilted but not browned. Stir in the zucchini and over high heat, shake the pan so the squash mixes with the onion and starts wilting, about 5 minutes. Sprinkle with salt, nutmeg, and pepper and add the bay leaf. Cover, reduce the heat, and cook for 10 minutes, stirring once in a while until the squash loses volume. Add the water with the dissolved bouillon cubes. Cover and simmer for 15 minutes.

Purée the soup right in the soup pot with an immersion blender or cool the squash before puréeing it in a blender or a food processor. Reheat the purée with the milk until it starts to boil. Whisk in the semolina in a steady stream and whisk for several minutes until the soup takes on a creamy texture. Add the cream and the butter. Taste and correct seasoning. Refrigerate and serve cold with fresh minced dill as a garnish.

# vichyssoise

The classic French leek and potato soup is very good cold. In the States, it is known as vichyssoise. The French had never heard of vichyssoise. Louis Diat left his hometown of Vichy in France to work as the chef of the Ritz Carlton in New York City, where he embellished the lowly potato and leek soup of his parents into a sophisticated soup for his rich clientele. He substituted chicken broth, milk, and cream for the water in the original recipe (see Classic French Leek and Potato Soup, page 14) and decorated the soup with chives.

6 leeks, white part only, thinly sliced (5 cups)

4 tablespoons (1/4 cup) butter

1/2 pound small Russet potatoes, peeled and halved (about 1 1/2 cups)

1 medium onion, peeled and sliced (1 cup)

1 tablespoon salt

Freshly ground black pepper

4 cups Chicken Broth (page 3), or a commercial broth or bouillon cubes

4 cups milk (whole, 2%, or 1%)

1/2 cup cream or half-and-half

1/4 teaspoon minced chives

Cut off all the green leaves of the leeks and keep them to make broth. Cut the whites lengthwise twice up to 1/2 inch of the stems. Open up the leaves of the leeks just like a flower, and under cold running water discard any dirt. Slice the leeks into 1-inch pieces.

In a 9-quart heavy-bottomed pot, melt the butter. When it starts sizzling, stir in the leeks, potatoes, and onion. Sprinkle with salt and pepper. Cover, reduce the heat, and braise for 15 minutes or until the leeks and onion are wilted, stirring and once in a while checking that nothing is burning. If the vegetables stick to the bottom of the pot, add about 1/4 cup water.

Pour the broth and the milk over the vegetables. Bring to a boil, cover, reduce the heat, and simmer for 45 minutes.

Purée the soup very quickly in a blender or food processor so the potatoes will not get gummy. Taste and correct seasoning. Strain the soup through a sieve to obtain a fine texture for the soup. Refrigerate.

When ready to serve, add the cream and more broth to thin the soup, if necessary.

Pour into chilled soup plates. Sprinkle with chives.

# gazpacho

Here are two gazpachos with practically the same ingredients but made with different techniques. In one, tomatoes are puréed with oil and vinegar and the soup is served with diced cucumber, onion, and pepper. For the second, the vegetables are all puréed with herbs. Melchior's Gazpacho is very pretty to look at and is very refreshing; Christina's has a more complex taste. I prefer soup plates to soup bowls—they offer a larger surface for the condiments.

# melchior's gazpacho

A friend of mine is married to Melchior, a Spaniard from Barcelona. During the summer, his gazpacho is a favorite of all my family.

4 pounds very ripe tomatoes

2 cups loosely packed bread, from the doughy part of the bread, not the crust, or Pullman Bread (page 164)

1 garlic clove, peeled and puréed

4 tablespoons red wine vinegar

½ cup olive oil

2 teaspoons salt or more

Freshly ground black pepper

1 medium onion, diced (1 cup)

1 small cucumber, peeled and diced (1 cup)

1 green bell pepper, diced (1 cup)

2 hard-boiled eggs, diced

Croutons (page 161)

Dice 2 tomatoes and reserve for the garnish. Soak the remaining tomatoes in boiling water for 10 seconds. Drain, peel, and chop.

Soak the bread in water for 5 minutes. Squeeze out the water and mix the bread with the tomatoes.

Purée the tomatoes, bread, and garlic in a food processor until very smooth. Strain the mixture through a fine-meshed sieve to remove the tomato seeds. Whisk in 3 table-spoons of the vinegar, then drizzle the olive oil into the tomato mixture. Sprinkle with salt and pepper and stir the gazpacho. Refrigerate.

Soak the onion in the remaining tablespoon vinegar for 30 minutes.

Refrigerate the diced vegetables and eggs in separate bowls.

Just before serving, prepare the croutons.

To serve, taste the soup and correct the seasoning. If the soup is too thick, add ice cubes to thin it out. Pour the tomato soup into chilled soup plates. Serve the diced vegetables and croutons on the side.

# christina's gazpacho

Herbs are mixed in this version of gazpacho and all the vegetables are puréed. The black olives are an essential part of the garnish—they give zest to the soup, which makes the dish special.

1 medium onion, peeled and chopped (1 cup)

1 cucumber, peeled and sliced (2 cups)

1 red bell pepper, chopped (1 cup)

1 garlic clove, peeled and chopped

1 1/2 pounds ripe tomatoes, chopped (4 1/2 cups)

2 cups loosely packed bread, not with the crust, or Pullman Bread (page 164)

1 tablespoon chopped parsley

1 tablespoon chopped fresh mint

1 tablespoon olive oil

1 tablespoon red wine vinegar

1 tablespoon finely ground almonds

Salt

Freshly ground white pepper

**For the Garnish:**

1 medium onion, diced (1 cup)

1/2 cucumber, peeled and diced (1 cup)

1 green pepper, diced (1 cup)

2 hard-boiled eggs, diced

1/2 cup chopped pitted black olives

In a large bowl, mix the vegetables (not the garnish), bread, herbs, oil, vinegar, and ground almonds. Process the mixture in a food processor in several batches. Sprinkle with salt and to taste. Strain the soup through a tamis (sieve) to give it a creamy consistency; add ice water to thin it if necessary. Refrigerate the soup and the garnish.

To serve, pour the soup into chilled soup plates and place garnishes nearby. Have each guest sprinkle the chosen garnishes on top.

# creamy white bean soup with tomatoes and tarragon

You can make this soup all through the year, eating it cold in the summer, hot in the winter. Cook fresh cranberry beans and fresh tomatoes during the summer, and use dried beans and canned tomatoes when the tomato season is over.

Drizzle some very fruity olive oil or truffle oil on top of the soup for a garnish.

1/4 cup olive oil

3 cups fresh cranberry beans or 3 cups parboiled navy or cannellini beans (see page 78)

6 garlic cloves, peeled and quartered

1 pound fresh tomatoes, chopped, or 1 (28-ounce) can Italian plum tomatoes, drained and chopped

3 large sprigs of tarragon
or 1 teaspoon dry tarragon

Freshly ground black pepper

6 cups water

1 tablespoon salt

Drizzle of a very fruity olive (summer)
or truffle oil (winter)

Heat the olive oil in a 9-quart pot, add the parboiled beans, garlic, and tomatoes. Bury the tarragon sprigs in the beans or sprinkle the dried tarragon in the beans and stir. Season with pepper. Cover and cook over medium heat for 10 minutes, stirring once in a while.

Pour the water over the beans and tomatoes. Bring to a light boil, cover, and cook at a gentle boil for 1 hour or more until the beans are very tender. Toward the end, season the beans with salt and more pepper. Cool the soup before the next step and discard the sprigs of tarragon.

In several batches, purée the soup in a blender or food processor until very smooth. Be sure the beans are tender or you won't get a smooth purée, or pass the soup through a sieve.

In the summer, serve the soup at room temperature (if it's too cold, it loses flavor). Drizzle a very fruity olive oil on top of each serving. In the winter, serve hot with truffle oil.

# pistou soup

When summer is in full swing, most cooks in southeastern France prepare *soupe au pistou*. It's similar to a minestrone served with *pistou*, a mix of basil, tomatoes, cheese, and oil. When the *pistou* is added to the vegetable soup just before serving it, the soup is transformed from an ordinary vegetable soup to a glorious one bursting with summer flavors. The ideal way to make this soup is to have a crowd of friends all helping to prepare it, for it takes a long time to dice the vegetables into small pieces. I tried cutting the vegetables in a food processor and the result was not great. The *pistou* is best made in a mortar. These time-consuming steps yield a sublime soup, celebrating the summer months.

**For the Soup:**

1 1/2 pounds potatoes,
diced into 1/4-inch cubes (3 cups)

1/2 pound fresh cranberry beans (2 cups)
or 1 1/3 cup parboiled navy or cannellini beans
(see page 78)

1/2 pound green beans,
cut into 1/4-inch slices (2 cups)

1/2 pound zucchini,
cut into 1/4-inch cubes (2 cups)

2 1/2 ounces white of leek,
cut into 1/4-inch slices (1 cup)

1/2 pound carrots,
cut into 1/4-inch cubes (2 cups)

15 cups water

3 tablespoons salt

1/2 pound fresh green peas

4 ounces canned chickpeas, drained

1/2 cup penne pasta

**For the Pistou:**

5 medium garlic cloves

2 cups fresh basil leaves

1 pound tomatoes, peeled and seeded

3/4 cup olive oil

2 cups freshly grated Gruyère cheese

1 teaspoon salt

**The soup:** Place all the vegetables except the green peas and chickpeas in a 9-quart heavy-bottomed pot. Add the water, sprinkle with salt, cover, and cook for 1 hour or until the vegetables are tender.

Add the green peas, chickpeas, and pasta; bring to a boil again. Cook until the pasta is tender, about 10 minutes.

**The pistou:** In a mortar with a pestle, mash the garlic with the basil and tomatoes. Beat the oil in gradually and add the cheese to make a thick paste. Season with salt.

At the last minute, add the *pistou* to the boiling soup. Stir all the ingredients and serve boiling hot.

**VARIATION:**

Add 1 pound of pancetta or bacon trimmed of most of the fat to cook with the soup.

# gardener's summer squash soup

This soup is best made with huge zucchini, those forgotten in gardens and grown to monstrous proportions. Madame Delubac makes this soup every year for the gastronomic festival in her village of Cairanne, in Provence. It's a big hit and good hot or cold.

6 pounds summer squash

$1/4$ cup olive oil

3 medium onions, peeled and sliced (3 cups)

1 teaspoon salt

Freshly ground black pepper

1 chicken bouillon cube

$1/2$ cup heavy cream

Fresh basil leaves, shredded for garnish

Peel the squash and cut it into $1/2$-inch-thick slices.

In a 9-quart heavy-bottomed pot, heat the olive oil over medium heat. Stir in the onions, cover, reduce the heat, and braise for 5 minutes.

Add the squash, which will fill the pot. Raise the heat to medium-high and stir the onions and squash together the best you can, watching that the onions do not burn. You must stir continually for several minutes until the squash starts rendering its liquid. Sprinkle with salt and pepper. Cover the pot, reduce the heat, and braise for 15 minutes or until the squash has melted to half its volume.

When the squash is soft, there should be enough liquid to cover it; if not add water to barely cover. Add a bouillon cube to give more flavor to the squash liquid. Cover the soup pot and simmer for 15 minutes. Cool.

In batches, purée the soup in a blender or food processor, or with an immersion blender. Add the cream and reheat the soup; taste and correct seasoning before serving it, garnished with basil.

To serve cold, cool before refrigerating for several hours.

# fresh corn soup with basil and garlic

This soup is a creation of the chef-owner of Etats Unis, a very nice bistro in New York City. If you are not cooking fresh corn right away, refrigerate it in its husk as soon as you have bought it, but try to eat it the same day as purchased. There are so many local farms today, it should not be difficult to buy fresh corn that's just been picked.

6 ears of corn

6 cups water

2 teaspoons salt

Freshly ground black pepper

1 cup basil leaves, loosely packed

2 garlic cloves

1 tablespoon butter

Stand the corn in a soup plate and cut off the kernels with a sharp knife but leave a thin layer of pulp on the cob; avoid cutting off tough cob fibers.

Bring the water to a boil in a 4-quart saucepan. Add the corn kernels and season with salt and pepper. Bring to a boil once more. Cover, lower the heat, and simmer until the corn is cooked; it should be no more than 5 minutes for very fresh corn.

In several batches, purée the corn with its liquid in a blender or food processor. If the soup is too thick, thin it with milk and force through a sieve if the soup is not smooth. Taste the soup and correct seasoning.

While reheating the soup, mash the basil, garlic, and butter in a mortar. Add 1 teaspoon of the mashed mixture at the bottom of each soup plate and pour the hot soup over it.

# pea and lettuce soup

Ruth Ziegler, an art dealer friend, gives wonderful parties for her clients. One of her summer menus always includes this soup, eaten either cold or hot. She makes the soup with tiny peas, called *petits pois*, from a can. There is very little work, a plus in hot weather. Choose the lettuce you like best but be sure to remove the stems from watercress and arugula, or the tough center rib of a Romaine. The soup improves after a few days in the refrigerator.

$^1/_2$ cup parsley leaves

4 cups chopped lettuce

1 14-ounce can tiny peas

$1^1/_2$ cup Chicken Broth (page 3),
or a commercial broth or bouillon cubes

1 cup heavy or light cream

Salt

$^1/_4$ teaspoon hot curry powder

$^1/_4$ cup minced chives

Croutons (page 161)

Combine the parsley, lettuce, peas with their liquid, and $^1/_2$ cup broth in the bowl of a food processor. Process until smooth.

Transfer the mixture to a 4-quart pot. Add the remaining broth and the cream. Bring to a slow boil. Season with salt and hot curry. Cover and simmer for 10 minutes.

Cool. Taste and adjust seasoning. Refrigerate if it is to be served cold. Decorate each bowl of soup with minced chives. Serve the croutons on the side.

# eggplant and red pepper soup with feta cheese

I had leftovers of an eggplant-pepper dish and was wondering what to do with them when inspiration struck: I poured my chicken broth over it (substitute a vegetable broth if you wish) and had a fabulous soup.

4 large red peppers

2 pounds eggplants (white or Japanese),
cut into 1/4-inch-thick slices (8 cups)

4 tablespoons olive oil

2 medium onions, thinly sliced (2 cups)

2 garlic cloves, minced

1/2 cup packed basil leaves or more if necessary

1 1/2 teaspoons salt

Freshly ground black pepper

1 cup or more crumbled feta cheese

6 cups Chicken Broth (page 3),
Vegetable Broth (page 5), or a commercial broth
or bouillon cubes

Char the peppers on top of the stove or under a broiler. Place them in a sturdy plastic bag and set aside to cool.

Peel the peppers the best you can over a large bowl. Cut them into quarters, then discard the seeds, ribs, and stems. Cut each quarter into 2 by 3-inch pieces. (I discard the juices generally because most of the time they taste bitter, but that's a matter of taste; reserve the juices if you wish for baking the dish.)

Preheat the oven to 350 degrees.

Bring a large amount of water to a boil in a 9-quart heavy-bottomed pot. Blanch the eggplants until the slices are soft, 5 to 10 minutes. Drain and let sit in the colander for 10 minutes.

Heat 2 tablespoons olive oil in a nonstick skillet over medium heat. Add the onions and garlic. Cover and braise for 5 minutes, taking care not to burn the onions. Scatter the onion-garlic mixture in the bottom of an oiled 3-quart baking dish. Tightly overlap the eggplants and pepper slices alternately in one row, and between each row add one or two basil leaves, then sprinkle with salt and pepper. Drizzle the remaining 2 tablespoons olive oil over the vegetables (add the pepper juices if you have kept them). Bake for 30 minutes in the middle of the oven.

Sprinkle the crumbled feta cheese over the vegetables and bake until the cheese melts, about 5 minutes or so. (The dish can be prepared ahead of time up to this point; when ready to serve, cover the dish with aluminum foil and reheat in a 300-degree oven for 15 minutes.)

Bring the broth to a boil and pour it into a tureen that you've heated with hot water. Bring the broth to the table along with the vegetable dish. Place a portion of vegetables in each soup bowl and cover with a ladle of broth.

# ratatouille soup with tagliatelle

I love ratatouille, a vegetable stew from southeastern France. When ratatouille season arrives—that is, when eggplants, zucchini, tomatoes, and peppers are in all the markets—I start making it practically every week. I make soup, or serve it as a vegetable or as a salad; so far, I have not found a way to make it into a dessert. When making ratatouille, be sure to boil down the vegetable liquids to concentrate their flavors, even for soup. Ratatouille is best eaten the next day or the day after, as it develops more flavor the longer it sits, but in my house when I want to have leftover ratatouille for a soup, I have to put notes such as "Danger" on it; otherwise it's eaten up before I can make the soup.

**For the Ratatouille:**

⅓ cup olive oil

2 medium onions, peeled, cut into 4 slices, then cut crosswise into 1-inch cubes (2 cups)

1 large red pepper, quartered, seeded, cut in strips, and cut into 1-inch cubes (1 cup)

2 garlic cloves, peeled and sliced

Sea salt

Pinch of cayenne (optional)

3 small zucchini, quartered lengthwise, then cut crosswise into 1-inch cubes (3 cups)

2 small eggplants (white or Japanese), cut lengthwise in thirds then crosswise into 1-inch cubes (4 cups)

5 large tomatoes (not the plum tomatoes), cut in eighths, then crosswise into 1-inch cubes (4 cups)

1 sprig of fresh mint

1 tablespoon salt

Freshly ground black pepper

**For the Broth:**

5 cups Chicken Broth or more (page 3), Vegetable Broth (page 5), or a commercial broth or bouillon cubes

**For the Pasta:**

½ pound tagliatelle pasta

3 tablespoons olive oil

Grated rind of 1 lemon

Salt

Freshly ground black pepper

A bowl of freshly grated Gruyère or Parmesan cheese

**The ratatouille:** Heat the oil in a 9-quart heavy-bottomed pot. Add the onions, pepper, and garlic and sir the vegetables for 1 minute. Sprinkle with 1 teaspoon salt and the cayenne pepper. Cover, reduce the heat, and braise for 15 minutes.

Stir in the zucchini. Cover and braise for another 10 minutes.

Add the eggplant and tomatoes, then sprinkle with more salt and cayenne to taste. Bury the mint in the vegetables; cover and braise for another 30 minutes or until the eggplant and tomatoes are soft and the vegetables have rendered their liquids. Drain the vegetables in a fine-meshed strainer placed over a large bowl.

Pour the liquids back into the soup pot and boil them down; once in a while, add the collected liquid in the large bowl under the vegetables. Boil down until the liquid becomes very syrupy. Discard the mint and stir the vegetables into the syrup. Taste and correct seasoning with more salt and pepper.

**The broth:** Bring the broth to a boil.

**The pasta:** Bring a large pot of salted water to a boil. Add the tagliatelle and cover; when the liquid returns to the boil, uncover and cook according to the instructions on the package.

Put 3 tablespoons olive oil in a large serving bowl with the lemon rind. Drain the pasta and toss it with the olive oil and lemon. Season with salt and freshly ground pepper.

Bring the ratatouille, broth, pasta, and grated cheese to the table in separate bowls. Serve the pasta first, the ratatouille, and then a ladle full of hot broth. Sprinkle with cheese and serve.

# bean, split pea, + lentil soups

## ON BEANS

During the winter months, I cook with dried beans, which I parboil and keep in the freezer for the many recipes I make with them, including soups. It's time-consuming to soak and parboil beans, so it's useful to have them ready when you want them. You can, of course, use canned beans, but dried are better, especially for soups that call for a sizable quantity of bean liquid. I soak the beans overnight in a large amount of water; the next day, I bring them to a boil in their soaking water. Once the boil is reached, I drain the beans; when cool, I put them in freezer bags and freeze them until I need them. It's not necessary to defrost the beans. One pound of dried beans equals 2 to $2^{1}/_{4}$ cups. After soaking and parboiling, 1 pound yields about 6 cups and when totally cooked between 7 and 8 cups. Navy and cannellini beans swell a little more than black beans.

# 3

Fresh cranberry beans are found in summer and early fall. They freeze very well; shell and freeze in freezer bags. One cup of fresh beans equals more or less 1 cup of pre-cooked dry beans. White, black, and red beans are Wayne's favorite food—any food as long as it's not green; to my despair he won't eat green beans.

Always buy beans from a greengrocer or supermarket that does a brisk business and has a rapid turnover.

## ON PARBOILING AND COOKING BEANS

Since Wayne likes beans so much, I keep bags of parboiled beans in the freezer and a pot of cooked beans in the refrigerator; that way he can indulge his bean craving and add cooked beans to soups. This recipe is for all kinds of beans: black, red, white, navy, or cannellini, or the French bean called *flageolet*.

# prepared dried beans

1 pound dried black, red, white, navy,
or cannellini beans

2 tablespoons olive or vegetable oil

1 medium onion,
quartered and stuck with 4 whole cloves

2 garlic cloves, crushed

6 cups water

3 sprigs of fresh thyme or 1 teaspoon dried thyme

1 tablespoon salt

**Parboiled beans:** Soak the beans overnight in a large amount of water in a 6-quart pot.

Bring the beans slowly to a boil in their soaking water. When the boil is reached, drain the beans. The parboiled beans are now ready to be cooked or can be frozen until ready to cook completely for the soups in this chapter.

**Cooked beans:** Heat the oil in a 6-quart heavy-bottomed pot. Stir in the onion, garlic, and beans and cook over medium heat for 5 minutes, stirring occasionally.

Pour in the water and add the thyme. Bring to a boil. Reduce the heat and cook at a gentle boil, covered, for 1 to 1 ½ hours or until the beans are tender. Check the beans once in a while to be sure there is enough liquid in the pot to prevent burning the beans at the bottom of the pan. Toward the end of the cooking time, add the salt.

Taste and correct the seasoning before serving the beans, or keep the beans refrigerated or frozen for soups that call for cooked beans, such as Basque Cabbage and Bean Soup (page 83), Bean and Squash Soup (page 84), or Sausage, Chickpea, and Potato Soup (page 124).

# black bean and tomato soup

In my winter dinner-party menus, including Christmas dinner, I often choose this elegant version of my friend Arlette Brisson's black bean soup. I make the soup a day ahead of time. I cook the ham hock broth at least a week before and freeze it. I also soak and parboil the beans ahead of time, cutting down on the work of preparing a menu with several courses. I garnish the soup with cherry tomatoes, avocado slices, and sour cream, which make the soup very festive.

2 tablespoons olive oil

4 medium onions, chopped (4 cups)

5 garlic cloves, finely chopped

3 (14-ounce) cans chopped Italian tomatoes with their juice

4 teaspoons ground cumin

4 teaspoons ground coriander

4 teaspoons dried oregano

1 bay leaf

6 cups parboiled black beans (see page 78)

1 tablespoon tomato purée

Few drops of Tabasco

1 cup chopped cilantro

2 1/2 quarts Smoked Ham Hock Broth (page 80)

1 tablespoon salt

Freshly ground black pepper

**For the Garnish:**

Sour cream

1 avocado, peeled and diced

8 cherry tomatoes, cut into halves

Heat the olive oil in a 9-quart pot. Add the onions and garlic. Cover, reduce the heat, and braise for 5 minutes without coloring. Add 2 or 3 tablespoons water to the onions to make sure they do not burn. Add the tomatoes, cumin, coriander, oregano, and bay leaf. Cover and braise for 10 minutes.

Stir in the beans, tomato purée, Tabasco, cilantro, and broth. Bring to a boil, cover, reduce the heat, and simmer for 3 hours. Toward the end of the cooking time, add the salt and pepper.

Cool. Discard the bay leaf. Purée half the soup in several batches in the blender until very smooth and pour it back into the soup pot. Refrigerate the soup until you need it.

Just before serving, while reheating the soup, prepare the garnish. Taste the soup and correct seasoning. Ladle the soup into individual warm soup bowls or soup plates. Garnish the soup with the sour cream, avocado, and cherry tomatoes.

# smoked ham hock broth

This broth is principally for the Black Bean and Tomato Soup on page 79, but it is a delicious broth for bean, cabbage, or lentil soups.

1 3-pound smoked ham hock

6 quarts cold water

3 celery stalks, chopped
(2 cups with 1/2 cup chopped celery leaves)

1 medium white turnip, sliced (1 cup)

2 carrots, sliced (2 cups)

2 small onions,
quartered and stuck with 4 whole cloves

Several sprigs of fresh parsley

1 leek with light green leaves, washed

3 garlic cloves

1 bay leaf

Sea salt

Place the ham hock and water in a 15-quart stockpot. Bring to a boil and add all the vegetables and seasoning. Reduce the heat and cook at a gentle boil, partially covered, for 3 hours.

Remove the ham hock from the broth; when it is cool enough to handle, cut off the fat and reserve the meat for a lunch or for leftover Black Bean and Tomato Soup (page 79).

Strain the broth through a sieve lined with cheesecloth placed over a large bowl. Let the broth cool before refrigerating for several hours.

Remove the fat from the broth by running a knife around the edge of the container and lifting off the fat with a wide spatula. Freeze the broth until ready to make the soup.

# spanish black bean soup

This is my everyday black bean soup—easy to make and can be made ahead of time. I make this soup for my family and the Black Bean and Tomato Soup (page 79) for special occasions.

6 cups parboiled black beans (see page 78)

2 medium onions, thinly sliced (2 cups)

8 cups water

Salt

2 tablespoons olive oil

1 red bell pepper, cored and cubed

4 garlic cloves, mashed

$^1/_2$ cup dry white wine, dry vermouth, or dry sherry

1 teaspoon dried oregano

1 teaspoon ground cumin

$^1/_4$ teaspoon sugar

Toast (page 160)

Put the beans in a 6-quart pot with 1 cup of the sliced onions. Pour in the water and bring to a boil. Cover, reduce the heat, and simmer for 1$^1/_2$ hours or until the beans are soft. Toward the end of the cooking time, season with salt.

Meanwhile, in a large nonstick skillet, heat the oil and stir in the remaining cup of onions, the bell pepper, and garlic. Sprinkle with $^1/_2$ teaspoon salt. Add about $^1/_2$ cup water and bring to a boil. Cover, reduce the heat, and braise for 15 minutes or until the water has evaporated and the vegetables are soft.

Drain the beans and reserve the bean liquid separately. You should have about 6 cups of beans and 5 to 6 cups of liquid. Purée 3 cups of the beans in several batches in a blender with 2 cups of the bean liquid.

Combine the puréed beans with the whole beans in the soup pot, then add the remaining bean liquid and the wine. Add the pepper-onion mixture. Sprinkle with oregano, cumin, and sugar. Taste and correct seasoning with salt if necessary. Serve with toast.

# bean and kale soup

If you have some pre-cooked beans in the freezer, as I generally have, this soup takes no time at all to make for your family, and it can be made ahead of time. When you buy kale, select bright, dark green leaves; avoid wilted green or yellowing leaves.

1 pound kale, collards, or dandelions

3 tablespoons olive oil

1 medium onion,
peeled and finely chopped (1 cup)

3 large garlic cloves,
peeled and coarsely chopped (1 1/2 tablespoons)

6 cups parboiled red beans (see page 78)

8 cups Chicken Broth (page 3),
Vegetable Broth (page 5), or a commercial broth
or bouillon cubes

1 tablespoon salt

A bowl of grated Parmesan cheese,
or cheese to grate at the table

Wash the kale and discard the thick stem. Shred the greens (10 cups, loosely packed).

Heat the oil in a 6-quart heavy-bottomed pot over medium heat. Stir in the onion and garlic, cover, reduce the heat, and braise for 10 minutes. Stir in the kale, cover, and braise for another 10 minutes.

Add the beans to the pot and pour in the broth. Bring to a boil, cover, reduce the heat, and cook at a gentle boil for 1 hour. Toward the end of the cooking time, add the salt.

Taste and correct seasoning. Serve the hot soup with the grated cheese on the side.

# basque cabbage and bean soup

Evelyn and Osa are two of my friends who spent one autumn in my house in Provence. Evelyn brought with her *espellette,* a seasoning named for the small Basque town where it originates. It's a mild chile, slightly larger than a jalapeño. I would say the taste is a cross between hot paprika and cayenne pepper—IGO Foods in San Francisco imports it (P.O. Box 77878, San Francisco, CA 94107; tel: 415-567-4796).

2 ½ pounds savoy cabbage

3 tablespoons olive oil

2 medium onions, sliced

6 garlic cloves, peeled and sliced

2 teaspoons ground, dried chile or espelette

1 ½ pounds Russet potatoes, peeled and cut into ½-inch cubes

1 tablespoon salt

3 quarts water

2 cups cooked white navy or cannellini beans (see page 78) or canned

Discard the tough dark green leaves of the cabbage, then quarter and cut out the stem. Cut each piece into thin slices.

In a 6-quart heavy-bottomed pot, heat the oil over medium heat and stir in the onions. Cover, reduce the heat, and braise for 5 minutes without coloring. Stir in the garlic and chile and braise for another 5 minutes.

Add the cabbage and potatoes. Sprinkle with salt; stir and add the water. Bring to a boil, cover, reduce the heat, and simmer for 1 hour.

Add the cooked beans and reheat the soup; taste and correct seasoning before serving.

# bean and squash soup

This is a very easy vegetarian soup that can be made with pumpkin, butternut, or banana squash. It can be made ahead of time, but prepare the *persillade,* a mixture of minced parsley and garlic, just before serving the soup.

3 tablespoons olive oil

1 large onion, peeled and sliced (1 ¹/₂ cups)

1 teaspoon ground espelette (see page 83) or 1 tablespoon minced mild chile

3 cups parboiled white or cannellini beans (see page 78)

2 pounds squash, peeled and cut into ¹/₂-inch cubes (6 cups)

9 cups water

1 tablespoon salt

Several sprigs of parsley

4 garlic cloves, peeled

In a 6-quart heavy-bottomed pot, heat the oil over medium heat. Add the onion and sprinkle with espelette or chile. Cover, reduce the heat, and braise for 10 minutes. Add the beans, squash, and water. Bring to a boil, cover, reduce the heat, and simmer for 1 ¹/₂ hours or until the beans are tender. Season with salt toward the end of the cooking time.

Just before serving, mince the parsley and garlic together (if you mince beforehand, you lose the parsley aroma from the parsley). Serve the soup very hot and garnish with the minced parsley and garlic.

# german potato and bean soup

My friend Inge Wilkenson is a natural cook and never measures anything. When I told her I was writing a soup cookbook she instantly told me she made very good soups; I believed her. I just had to be alert while she cooked her soups so I could measure the ingredients before she slipped one in on me. We cooked the soup in the morning and reheated it for dinner.

4 tablespoons olive oil

1/2 pound slab bacon, cut into small pieces

2 medium onions, finely chopped (1 cup)

1 celery stalk, diced small (1/2 cup)

2 pounds potatoes, diced small (4 cups)

2 carrots, sliced (1 cup)

4 cups parboiled navy or cannellini beans (see page 78)

10 cups Chicken Broth (page 3), Vegetable Broth (page 5), or a commercial broth or bouillon cubes

Several sprigs of fresh parsley

3 bay leaves

Few grinds of the pepper mill

Salt

3 tablespoons white vinegar

Heat the olive oil in a 9-quart heavy-bottomed pot over medium heat and add the bacon. Fry until lightly brown, stirring occasionally; do not burn. Transfer to a plate. Stir in the onions and celery and cook, stirring occasionally, for about 5 minutes.

Add the potatoes, carrots, beans, bacon, and broth to the pot. Bury the parsley in the soup. Add the bay leaves and pepper. Bring to a boil, cover, reduce the heat, and simmer gently for about 1 1/2 hours or until the beans are cooked. With a long-handled spoon, from time to time skim off and discard the fat from the top of the simmering soup. Toward the end of the cooking time, add salt to taste.

Discard the parsley and add the vinegar just before serving.

# fresh cranberry bean soup

In New York City, where I live part time, I find fresh cranberry beans—sometimes called September beans—in our farmers' markets. I also freeze batches of shelled beans and keep them in plastic bags. In the summer, I prefer using fresh beans—they are more meaty than the dry ones.

What makes this soup special is the raw garlic mashed with lots of basil leaves, which is added to the soup at the last minute. The aroma as well as the taste is so fresh. The addition of freshly grated Gruyère cheese makes a very special soup; if possible, use Appenzeller, the most flavorful cheese from Switzerland.

Make the soup ahead of time but prepare the *pistou* (the mashed basil leaves and garlic) when reheating the soup.

1/3 cup olive oil

2 medium onions, thinly sliced (2 cups)

2 pounds tomatoes, peeled, seeded, and chopped (4 cups)

3 cups shelled fresh cranberry beans (2 to 2 1/2 pounds in the pods)

5 cups water

1 tablespoon salt

6 large garlic cloves, mashed

Fresh basil leaves (3 cups)

A large bowl of freshly grated Gruyère cheese

In a 6-quart heavy-bottomed pot, heat the oil over medium-high heat. Add the onions, cover, reduce the heat, and braise for 10 minutes.

Add the tomatoes, cover, and braise for 10 more minutes.

Add the beans and pour the water over the beans. Bring to a boil, cover, reduce the heat, and cook at a gentle boil for 1 to 1 1/2 hours or until the beans are tender. Add salt toward the end of the cooking time.

Just before serving, mash the garlic with a pestle in a large mortar. Add the basil and mash the basil into a purée. If you don't have a mortar, put the garlic through a press into a bowl and stir or mash in the minced basil. Add the pistou to the hot soup at the last minute. Taste and correct seasoning. Serve hot with Gruyère on the side.

Note: Substitute 2 1/2 cups parboiled beans and 2 cups drained canned tomatoes when the fresh beans are out of season.

# flageolet bean soup

This soup is part of my Thanksgiving repertoire. It is prepared ahead of time, which makes life easier when there is so much to do. You can find flageolets, a dried green bean, in many gourmet retailers or catalogues, or you can substitute dried navy beans.

3 cups parboiled flageolets beans (see page 78)

6 cups water

1 garlic clove, peeled

1 medium onion,
peeled and stuck with 3 whole cloves

2 teaspoons salt

3 cups Chicken Broth (page 3), Turkey Broth (page 4), Vegetable Broth (page 5), or a commercial broth or bouillon cubes

1 tablespoon fresh thyme leaves

1/2 cup heavy cream or half-and-half

Tomato Relish (page 88)

Croutons (page 161)

In a 6-quart heavy-bottomed pot, cover the beans with the water. Bury the garlic and onion in the beans. Bring to a boil, cover, reduce the heat, and simmer for 1 1/2 to 2 hours. Flageolets take longer to cook than navy beans. Toward the end of the cooking time, season with salt. When cooked, there should be very little water left in the pot. Drain and reserve the beans and liquid. Let cool.

In several batches, purée the beans with their liquid in a blender or food processor, adding some broth to each batch. Pour the soup back into the pot. Depending on how much water was left in the cooking, add enough broth to the desired soup consistency. Add the thyme and stir in the cream.

Just before serving, reheat the soup and add more broth in case the soup thickened too much while resting. Taste and correct seasoning with salt and freshly ground pepper. Garnish each soup bowl with tomato relish and serve the croutons on the side.

# tomato relish

This relish is great with all kinds of soups, especially my Thanksgiving soup of flageolets (see page 87). I make batches of it for the refrigerator.

| | |
|---|---|
| 8 shallots, peeled and finely chopped | In a mortar, mash the chopped shallots into a purée with the pestle. |
| 1 (14-ounce) can peeled Italian plum tomatoes | |
| ¼ cup olive oil | Drain the tomatoes (reserve the juice) and chop them coarsely. |
| Salt | |
| Freshly ground black pepper | Heat the oil in a large nonstick skillet. Add the shallots and tomatoes. Season with salt, pepper, and oregano. Cook over low heat, stirring occasionally. When the tomato mixture dries out, start adding ¼ cup of the reserved tomato juice at a time. Cook the tomatoes for 15 minutes or until the tomato mixture is thick. Refrigerate until ready to use. |
| 1 teaspoon oregano leaves | |

Just before serving it, reheat in a microwave or in a double boiler.

# ribollita
## minestrone and bread soup

You need to plan ahead for this Tuscan soup; first cook the beans, then sauté the vegetables for a second cooking with the beans. Finally, soak the bread in the soup for three hours and bring it back to a boil (*ribollita* means "reboiled"). Is it worth it? Yes. The soup is a perfect dish for a large crowd on a very cold day.

6 cups parboiled cannellini or navy beans (see page 78)

4 large garlic cloves, peeled

$1/2$ cup fresh sage leaves

3 quarts water

Salt

$1/4$ cup olive oil

2 medium onions, peeled and diced (2 cups)

2 celery stalks, diced (1 cup)

2 large carrots, peeled and diced (1 cup)

1 large Russet potato, peeled and diced (2 cups)

$1/4$ cup chopped parsley

A strip of lemon peel

1 (14-ounce) can peeled Italian plum tomatoes

1 small head savoy cabbage, core discarded and leaves shredded (8 cups)

1 teaspoon red pepper flakes

Freshly ground black pepper

4 cups 1-inch cubes of stale Tuscan Bread (page 158)

Olive oil, for the garnish

In a 9-quart heavy-bottomed pot, combine the beans, garlic, and sage, and pour the water over them. Bring to a boil, cover, reduce the heat, and simmer for 1 to 1 $1/2$ hours or until the beans are tender. Toward the end of the cooking of the beans, add 2 teaspoons salt.

Drain the beans, reserving the liquid (you should have at least 8 cups bean liquid; if not, add water). Purée half the beans with 2 cups of bean liquid either in a blender or food processor or with an immersion blender. Reserve the puréed beans, as well as the whole ones, with all the liquid in a large mixing bowl.

In the same pot, heat the olive oil over medium heat. Sauté the onions, celery, carrots, potato, and parsley for 5 minutes, stirring most of the time. Add the lemon peel, tomatoes with the juice, and cabbage. Sprinkle with red pepper flakes, 2 teaspoons salt, and the black pepper. Cover the pot and braise for 10 minutes, stirring occasionally.

Add the reserved beans and bean liquid, and bring to a boil. Cover, reduce the heat, and simmer with the liquid bubbling gently for another 1 $1/2$ hours, stirring occasionally. Turn off the heat and stir in the stale bread. Let the soup rest for at least 3 hours or the whole day, or overnight at room temperature.

Just before serving, bring the soup to a boil, taste, and correct the seasoning. Serve at once. Drizzle olive oil over the individual portions.

# jamaican yellow split pea soup

Cecily Brownstone, for many years food editor for the Associated Press, and I have often feasted during the winter on yellow split pea soup made by Alicia Campbell-Collins, Cecily's Jamaican helper.

1 pound yellow split peas

3 quarts Vegetable Broth (page 5)
or a commercial broth

1 1/2 cups sliced onions

2 large celery stalks, sliced 1/4 inch thick (1 cup)

2 medium carrots, sliced 1/4 inch thick (1 cup)

2 medium turnips, sliced 1/4 inch thick (1 cup)

1 parsnip, sliced 1/4 inch thick (1/2 cup)

1 large scallion

2 large sprigs of fresh thyme
or 1 teaspoon dried thyme

2 bay leaves

4 whole allspice

Salt

Freshly ground black pepper

Rinse the split peas under cold running water.

Put the yellow split peas in a 9-quart heavy-bottomed pot and cover them with the broth. Bring to a boil, cover, reduce the heat, and simmer for about 45 minutes.

Add the vegetables along with the herbs and spices. Cover and continue cooking with the liquid bubbling gently for 45 minutes or until the vegetables are very tender.

With a long-handled spoon, remove the thyme sprigs, bay leaves, and allspice—they will be quite visible—and discard. Cool the soup. Purée the soup in several batches in a blender or food processor, or use an immersion blender. Season with salt and freshly ground pepper to taste.

If the soup is thicker than you like, thin it with more broth. Reheat the soup; taste and correct seasoning with more salt and pepper.

# zen split pea and barley soup

At the Mountain Zen Center in Santa Rosa, California, this soup is made for large groups. Neil Myers, a regular at the center, gave me the proportions for 10, 20, 30, 40, and 50 people; I cut it down to serve eight. It's a substantial thick soup, best eaten as soon as it is cooked before it gets too thick, though you can, of course, thin it with more vegetable broth if you prepare it ahead of time.

1 cup split peas

1 medium onion, chopped

2 teaspoons celery seed

$1/2$ cup loosely packed chopped fresh basil or $1/2$ tablespoon dried basil

Several sprigs of fresh thyme or 1 tablespoon dried thyme

10 sprigs of parsley, chopped

2 teaspoons salt or more

Freshly ground black pepper

8 cups Vegetable Broth (page 5) or a commercial broth

$1/3$ cup pearled barley

Butter (optional)

In a 6-quart heavy-bottomed pot, combine the split peas, onion, and herbs; sprinkle with salt and pepper. Pour in the broth, bring to a boil, cover, reduce the heat, and simmer 1 hour.

Add the barley and simmer for another 30 minutes or until the barley and split peas are soft.

Taste and correct the seasoning before serving. Serve very hot, with a tablespoon of butter swirled into each soup bowl, if you wish.

# red lentil soup with curry

This is a soup Renee Behnke makes for her family. "Madame Sur La Table," as I affectionately call her, has given us all those beautiful cookware stores around the country—candy stores for cooks that she bought from the original owner, who started the business in Seattle. She makes her soup with chicken broth, but it is also very good with vegetable broth. The soup will thicken, prepared ahead of time; just thin it with more broth when reheating.

2 tablespoons vegetable oil

1 large onion, sliced (1 1/2 cups)

2 tablespoons minced garlic

2 tablespoons minced fresh ginger

2 tablespoons minced jalapeño pepper

1 1/2 tablespoons curry powder

1 1/2 teaspoons ground cinnamon

1 teaspoon ground cumin

2 bay leaves

8 ounces red lentils, rinsed (1 1/2 cups)

8 cups Chicken Broth (page 3), Vegetable Broth (page 5), or a commercial broth or bouillon cubes

3 tablespoons chopped fresh cilantro

2 tablespoons fresh lemon juice

2 tablespoons mango or tomato chutney

About 2 teaspoons salt

Freshly ground black pepper

1/3 cup sour cream or plain yogurt

In a 6-quart heavy-bottomed pot, heat the oil over medium heat. Stir in the onion, reduce the heat, and cook for a few minutes without burning the onion. Add the garlic, ginger, jalapeño, curry, cinnamon, cumin, and bay leaves and cook, stirring for 2 more minutes. Add the lentils and broth; bring to a boil. Cover, reduce the heat, and cook at a gentle boil for 45 minutes or until the lentils are cooked.

With tongs, fish out and discard the bay leaves. Stir in the cilantro, lemon juice, and chutney. Season with salt and pepper.

Just before serving, reheat the soup; if the soup is thicker than you like, thin it with more broth. Garnish the soup with dollops of sour cream or yogurt.

# georges blanc's green lentil soup with celery root

This soup comes from a Michelin three-star restaurant owned by Georges Blanc. In general, soups made in restaurants such as this are too complicated to realize in a home kitchen, but this one is easy to make and it's rich in taste but not rich in calories. It can be made ahead of time, too, making it a perfect beginning for a dinner party.

1 1/2 cups green or brown lentils

1/2 pound celery root

4 tablespoons olive oil

1 medium onion, coarsely chopped

1 medium leek, white part only, cleaned and cut into 1/4-inch slices (1 cup)

2 shallots, coarsely chopped

1 garlic clove, mashed with salt and freshly ground pepper

1 tablespoon salt

Freshly ground black pepper

8 cups Chicken Broth (page 3), Vegetable Broth (page 5), or a commercial broth or bouillon cubes

2 cups loosely packed watercress, stems removed

1 tablespoon Dijon mustard

1 1/2 tablespoons red wine vinegar

Heavy cream, for decoration (optional)

Cover the lentils with a generous amount of water in a 6-quart heavy-bottomed pot. Bring to a boil and keep a steady boil for 15 minutes. Drain the lentils and set aside.

Peel the celery root by slicing off the outside with a knife. Cut it into 1/4-inch cubes (1 cup).

Heat the olive oil in the soup pot; add the celery root, onion, leek, shallots, and garlic. Cover and braise over medium heat for 10 minutes.

Add the lentils to the vegetable mixture. Pour in the broth, season with salt and pepper, and bring to a boil. Reduce the heat, and cook at a gentle boil, partially covered, for 1 hour. During the last 5 minutes of cooking, add the watercress.

Purée the soup in batches in a blender until very smooth. (The food processor does not grind the skins of the lentils fine enough or, if you are processing, then pass through a fine-meshed sieve to discard the skins.) Add more broth if the soup is too thick. Whisk in the mustard and vinegar.

Just before serving, reheat the soup, taste, and correct seasoning with more salt and pepper. Ladle the soup into hot soup bowls or plates. Dribble the soup with heavy cream, if you wish.

# seafood *soups*

Thursday is fish day in Nyons; that's market day in
our little inland town; I rely on the fish and seafood brought in by our market vendors on
Thursday; the fish is fresh from the Mediterranean that day. We make soups
with seafood, especially with mussels, and of course when we have lots of
guests, we all make bouillabaisse.

All the seafood soups with mussels, clams, and oysters can be made ahead of
time, but remember to reheat the soup under the boil to keep the seafood
from toughening. The broth for the Mediterranean Fish Soup (bouillabaisse)
can be prepared ahead of time, as well as the *rouille* (the saffron-garlic
mayonnaise), but wait until dinnertime to poach the fish, and steam the
mussels at the same time as the fish is poached.

# 4

# cabbage soup with halibut

Romans and Greeks considered cabbage a miracle worker. It was reputed to purge the digestive system, to heal scars, to balance the nervous system, and to cure hangovers.

I like savoy cabbage, but another variety is fine, too. I prepare most of the soup ahead of time and poach the fish and cook the potatoes before dinnertime.

2 1/2 pounds savoy cabbage

4 tablespoons vegetable or olive oil

1 medium onion, peeled and quartered (1 cup)

3 thick slices of coppa or prosciutto,
cut in half (1 pound)

3 carrots, peeled,
each carrot cut into 3 pieces (2 cups)

2 medium turnips, peeled,
cut into 2-inch cubes (2 cups)

10 cups Chicken Broth (page 3),
Vegetable Broth (page 5), or a commercial broth
or bouillon cubes

Salt

Freshly ground black pepper

3 medium potatoes, peeled and quartered (3 cups)

1 1/2 pounds halibut steak

1 1/4 cups Rouille (page 99)

Poilane Bread (page 156) or
Tuscan Bread (page 158)

Discard the tough outer cabbage leaves; cut out and discard the stalk. Split the cabbage into six wedges, place in a 9-quart heavy-bottomed pot, and cover with cold water. Bring the water to a rolling boil and cook the cabbage for 5 minutes. Drain the cabbage in a colander set into the sink and rinse it with running cold water. Reserve.

Heat the oil in the same pot and stir in the onion. Cover the pot, reduce the heat, and braise the onion for 5 minutes or so without coloring it. Stir in the coppa or prosciutto, carrots, and turnips. Cover and braise once more for another 5 minutes. Add the cabbage and pour in the broth; season with salt and pepper. Bring to a boil, cover, reduce the heat, and simmer for 1 hour. (Soup up to this point can be prepared ahead of time.)

Before dinnertime, cover the potatoes with cold salted water and bring to a boil in a 4-quart pan. Cover, reduce the heat, and simmer for 20 minutes or until the potatoes are tender. Drain the potatoes (never leave cooked potatoes in water; they get water-logged). Transfer the potatoes to a preheated platter and keep in a warm oven.

Meanwhile, cover the halibut with salted cold water and bring slowly to a boil in a wide pan. Turn off the heat, cover the pot, and let sit for 5 minutes. Pierce the flesh of the halibut with a toothpick—if it goes in easily the fish is cooked. Drain, skin, and bone the fish. Cut into six pieces.

Serve the fish with the potatoes on the pre-heated platter along with the cabbage soup in a tureen, and a bowl of garlic mayonnaise and thick slices of bread to accompany.

# mediterranean fish soup with garlic mayonnaise

This soup has the delicate taste of saffron, the flavor that characterizes the fish soups of southeastern France. The broth is the most important element of the soup—it must be rich in flavor. In the United States, I make the broth with red snapper; in France, I buy a mixture of fish called *soupe de roche*, which is the basis of an authentic bouillabaisse. Poach any fish you like as long as it is not oily.

2 pounds monkfish, boned and cut into 8 pieces, or any white fish such as halibut, cod, or striped bass

Large pinch of saffron strands

1 tablespoon Pernod, a type of anisette

Salt

Freshly ground black pepper

2 pounds small red bliss potatoes, scrubbed

8 cups Fish Broth (page 6) made with red snapper

2 pounds mussels, scrubbed, any open shells discarded

Rouille (page 99)

Toast (page 160)

Place the fish on a platter and rub it with the saffron strands, drizzle the Pernod over the fish, and sprinkle with salt and pepper. Let stand for 30 minutes or so before poaching.

In a 4-quart pan, cover the potatoes with water and bring to a boil. Simmer until the potatoes are tender, about 20 minutes.

Meanwhile, bring the broth to a boil in a 9-quart pot. Add the fish and cover the pot tightly. Turn off the heat. Test the fish after 5 minutes by pricking with a toothpick.

While the fish is poaching, put the mussels in a large pot; cover the pan and place over high heat for a few minutes, shaking the pot once in a while. As soon as the shells open, turn off the heat. With a large wire-meshed skimmer, scoop out the mussels and transfer them to a large bowl. (Freeze the broth for another preparation such as Reboul's Mussel and Pasta Soup (page 102) or La Mouclade (page 103); it is generally too strong and salty and would overpower the subtle flavor of the red snapper broth.) Transfer the poached fish to a preheated platter and arrange the mussels around the fish. Place in a warm oven while reheating the broth.

To serve, place a piece of fish, potato, and a few mussels in their shells in individual preheated soup plates and pour the hot broth over it. Serve with the rouille on the side with toast.

# rouille
## garlic mayonnaise with saffron

This mayonnaise is good not only with fish soups but with raw vegetables as well. If you're serving it with vegetables, omit the fish broth and substitute water. I keep it refrigerated for several days. Always mix olive oil with vegetable oil—olive oil alone would be way too strong.

3 large garlic cloves, mashed to a purée

2 egg yolks

1/4 teaspoon powdered saffron

1/8 teaspoon turmeric

1/8 teaspoon hot paprika

1/2 teaspoon salt

1/16 teaspoon or more cayenne

1/2 cup olive oil

1/2 cup vegetable oil

3–4 tablespoons Fish Broth (page 6)

In the bowl of a heavy-duty mixer, combine the garlic, egg yolks, saffron, turmeric, paprika, salt, and cayenne. At medium speed, beat the mixture until smooth. Drop by drop, whisk in the oil; it takes about 10 minutes. Gradually, whisk in tablespoons of fish broth or water to smooth out the mayonnaise.

Taste and correct seasoning, adding salt and cayenne if necessary. Refrigerate the rouille for as long as four days.

# lobster bisque

I had read how to kill a lobster but I was too chicken to do it myself. Since I am very good at giving orders, I decided that Wayne would kill the lobster so I could retrieve the roe without cooking it first. (If you poach the lobster, the coral and tomalley might cook and not blend into the soup.)

First, I learned how to recognize a female from a male lobster—that was easy: the second appendages (swimmerets, or small flaps) found under the tail of the lobster are soft and feathery for a female, firm and rigid for a male; also, the female has a broader abdomen than the male. The hard part was killing the creature without cooking it. I had read somewhere to stroke the back of the lobster to hypnotize it. I don't know if it's true, but once on the cutting board, the lobster was quiet after I stroked it. Armed with a large kitchen knife, Wayne plunged it into the back where the head and body meet. From my reading, I learned that the lobster was killed instantly and if it still jiggled, it was just nerves (just like a chicken running around without its head) and it hadn't suffered. Well, I made Wayne do it, and it still jiggled, but he continued to dissect it, cutting off the head and tail, and separating the claws. He washed his hands and said to me, "Now you can cook."

He left the kitchen and I had just started cooking when I glimpsed a piece of paper on the table with Wayne's handwriting: Georgette the lobster had written me a small poem saying goodbye, and she hoped the soup would be delicious. I felt bad for her, but as Wayne said, it is perhaps better to be killed quickly with a knife than be boiled or eaten by a shark!

If you don't want to kill the lobsters yourself, ask the fishmonger to do it, but be sure that he dissects them inside a large pan so all the juices are not lost. You need them to make the soup.

When you buy female lobsters, be sure they weigh 2 pounds or more each; under 2 pounds the females are too young to have eggs.

2 (2-pound) female lobsters

5 tablespoons olive oil

1/4 cup cognac

3 tablespoons all-purpose flour

3 cups water

2 tablespoons tomato paste

2 cups white wine, such as Chardonnay

Salt

Several strands of saffron

Pinch of cayenne

Several sprigs of parsley

Freshly ground black pepper

1 cup heavy cream or half-and-half

Place each lobster on a cutting board with a groove for catching juices. You'll want to save all the juices that run out. Kill the lobster by severing the spinal cord. Plunge a sharp knife into the lobster at the joint where the head joins the body. Cut off the head at this joint and split it in two lengthwise. This allows you to locate the small sand sac between the eyes. Remove it and discard it.

At the point where the tail joins the body, you will find two green substances, one darker than the other. The darker substance, almost black, is the roe, which is found only in the female lobster. It will turn light red in cooking, hence the name "coral." The lighter green substance is the tomalley, or liver. Reserve both.

In a 9-quart, heavy-bottomed pot, heat 2 tablespoons of the olive oil and stir-fry the lobster pieces in several batches until the shells are red, adding more oil if necessary. Pour the cognac into the pot, light a match, and drop it in; the cognac should instantly ignite. Keep your face away from the pot and shake the pan until the flames subside. Transfer the lobster pieces to a large platter and reserve.

In the same pot, heat the remaining 3 tablespoons olive oil. Whisk in the flour and cook for 1 minute until smooth, stirring all the while. Whisk in the roe and tomalley, then pour in the water, the tomato paste diluted with the wine, the reserved lobster juices, salt, saffron, cayenne, parsley, and pepper. Bring to a boil once more, add the lobster pieces, cover the pot, reduce the heat, and simmer for 15 minutes.

With tongs, transfer the claws and tails to a platter. Shell the lobster pieces and reserve for later. Put the shells back in the pot. Cover the pot and simmer for 30 minutes more.

Discard the shells and heads. Strain the lobster soup through a fine-meshed sieve and with the back of a spoon, push down as hard as possible on the debris inside the strainer. Discard the debris.

Add the cream to the soup and bring to a simmer. Add the reserved lobster pieces, and heat below the boil for another 5 minutes to warm the lobster without toughening it. Taste and correct seasoning before serving the soup in heated soup bowls.

# reboul's mussel and pasta soup

J. B. Reboul lived at the end of the nineteenth and beginning of the twentieth centuries and is considered the most famous chef of French Provençal cooking. His book *La Cuisiniere Provencale* (The Provençal Cook) is still the bible. He recommends cooking rice or pasta in this soup. I chose fusilli, a pasta that cooks fast.

3 pounds mussels

1 small onion, finely chopped (1/2 cup)

2 cups water

1 bay leaf

3 tablespoons olive oil

1 leek, white part with the light green leaves, chopped (1 cup)

1 large pinch of saffron threads

1 cup pasta (fusilli)

Salt

Freshly ground black pepper

Scrub the mussels clean under running cold water with a wire brush. Place the mussels and onion in a 6-quart, heavy-bottomed pot with the water. Add the bay leaf. Cover and bring to a boil over high heat for 3 minutes or so or until the mussels are opened.

Drain the mussels in a strainer clamped over a bowl, reserving the liquid. Take the mussels from their shells and keep them in a bowl. Cover the bowl with a lid and place the bowl in a large pan with hot water like a *bain-marie* (a water bath). The mussels will keep warm but not overcook, covered in a hot water bath.

In the same pot, heat the oil and stir in the leek. Stir constantly until the leek starts to wilt, 3 to 4 minutes. Pour in the reserved mussel broth. Sprinkle with the saffron. Bring to a boil and add the pasta. Cover the pot to avoid evaporation and cook the pasta to al dente.

Add the mussels to the pasta. Taste and correct seasoning with salt and pepper.

Serve hot in soup bowls.

# la mouclade
## french mussel soup with curry

La Mouclade is a specialty of La Rochelle, a coastal town in western France, south of Brittany. In the eighteenth century, French merchants traded with India and discovered curry. The soup consists of a velouté sauce made with the mussel poaching liquids—white wine and the mussel liquor. It's easy to make and delicious as a first course for a dinner party (the soup can be prepared ahead of time) or as a main course with steamed potatoes.

3 pounds mussels

2 large shallots, quartered

1 ½ cups white wine, such as Chardonnay

Fish Broth (page 6) or water, as needed

2 tablespoons butter

3 tablespoons all-purpose flour

½ cup milk (whole, 2%, or 1%)

½ cup heavy cream or half-and-half

1 teaspoon mild curry

Salt

Steamed potatoes, quartered (optional)

Scrub the mussels clean with a wire brush under cold running water. Place the mussels, shallots, and wine in a 6-quart heavy-bottomed pot. Pour the wine over the mussels, cover, and bring to a boil as quickly as possible, shaking the pot once in a while. When the mussels open, turn off the heat. If some of the mussels remain closed, discard them.

Strain the mussels and their liquid through a fine-meshed sieve clamped on top of a large bowl. You should have 3 cups liquid; if not, add broth or water to make 3 cups. Pick out the shallots and reserve for later.

In the same pot, melt the butter; whisk in the flour and pour in the mussel liquid, being careful not to add the sand if there is any at the bottom of the liquid. Whisk in the milk, cream, and the reserved shallots and sprinkle with the curry. Cover and simmer for 30 minutes, whisking from time to time. Meanwhile, shell the mussels and add them to the soup with a few shells for the garnish.

When ready to eat, slowly reheat the soup. Taste and correct seasoning, adding more curry if you wish and salt if necessary. Sometimes, the mussel liquor is very salty, so be careful.

Serve accompanied with steamed potatoes if the soup is served as a main course.

# my christmas oyster and wild mushroom soup

During the holidays, I splurge with my favorite foods: oyster soup is one. I can prepare most of the soup ahead of time and just before dinner I poach the oysters. For a less festive dish, you can eliminate the egg yolk and cream enrichment.

To be sure that the oysters are fresh, have them shucked by the fishmonger; it's worth paying a bit more to keep your hands intact. Mr. DeMartino, my fishmonger of years ago in New York City, told me this sad tale: A customer of his, a surgeon, wanted to save money by learning how to open oysters. After impaling his right hand, he spent Christmas in the emergency room and was unable to operate for several weeks. His oysters were very dear!

24 shucked oysters and their liquor

10 exotic mushrooms, such as chanterelles or oyster mushrooms

4 tablespoons (1/4 cup) butter

3 tablespoons all-purpose flour

6 cups Fish Broth (page 6)

**For the Enrichment:**

3 egg yolks

1/2 cup heavy cream or half-and-half

Salt

Freshly ground black pepper

Strain the oysters in a sieve clamped over a mixing bowl. Quarter the oysters and reserve. Reserve the oyster liquid in a bowl.

Clean the mushrooms with a damp paper towel. Quarter them and reserve.

In a 6-quart heavy-bottomed pot, melt the butter and whisk in the flour for a minute. Whisk in the fish broth, then add the mushrooms. Cover, reduce the heat, and simmer at a gentle boil for 20 minutes.

Add the oyster liquor and simmer for another 5 minutes. Turn off the heat and let cool (can be done two to three hours ahead to this step).

Just before serving, combine the egg yolks with the cream in a mixing bowl and whisk it into the soup. Reheat the soup very slowly, whisking once in a while. When the soup is hot but not boiling, add the oysters, cover, and cook without boiling for 5 minutes. Taste and correct seasoning. Serve immediately with croutons.

# oyster soup

The oysters are poached in a court-bouillon (an acidulated poaching liquid for fish, seasoned with vegetables and cooked for a short time) and enriched with cream. It is a lighter soup than the preceding oyster soup.

Large pinch of saffron strands

1 cup half-and-half

3 cups Court-Bouillon (page 106)

36 shucked oysters with their liquor, quartered

Salt

Freshly ground black pepper

Seep the strands of saffron in the half-and-half for 30 minutes. In a 4-quart heavy-bottomed pot, combine the oyster liquor, court-bouillon, and saffron cream; bring slowly to a boil. Add the oysters and poach with the liquid bubbling very gently for 10 minutes. Taste and correct seasoning. Serve very hot.

# court-bouillon

3 cups water

2 1/2 cups white wine, such as Chardonnay

8 cherry tomatoes, halved

1 leek, white part only,
cut into 1-inch-thick slices (1/2 cup)

2 carrots, thinly sliced

1 celery stalk, thinly sliced

1 medium onion, quartered

3 garlic cloves, quartered

1/2 cup chopped flat parsley leaves

1 1/2 teaspoons salt

Freshly ground black pepper

Combine the water, wine, vegetables, and seasonings in a 4-quart heavy-bottomed pot. Bring to a boil, cover, reduce the heat, and simmer for 1 hour. Strain the court-bouillon. Refrigerate for a day or two, or freeze.

# steamers with their broth

I'll never forget my first trip to Boston where I managed to eat two quarts of steamers. Accompany the steamers with a good homemade crusty bread such as Tuscan bread (page 158). The unsalted bread is a good counterpart to the briny broth.

4–5 dozen steamers (3–4 pounds)

1 cup dry white wine (or water)

2 cups water

4 parsley sprigs, with stems

1 celery stalk, with leaves, coarsely chopped

3 bay leaves

8 tablespoons (1 stick) butter, melted

Tuscan Bread (page 158)

Soak the clams in plenty of cold salted water for 15 to 30 minutes; drain, soak for an additional 15 minutes. Scrub the clams with a wire brush under cold running water.

Put the wine and water in a 4-quart heavy-bottomed pot with the parsley, onion, celery, and bay leaves. Bring to a boil, lower the heat, and simmer for 5 to 10 minutes.

Add the clams, cover the pot, and boil briskly for 3 to 5 minutes until the clams open. As they open, remove with tongs to a serving bowl. Discard any clams that don't open.

Strain the broth into another bowl through a fine-mesh sieve lined with dampened cheese cloth. Discard the debris.

Serve the steamers with the broth and the melted butter. To eat, remove each clam from its shell, peel off the black membrane that runs down the side, and, holding the clam by the "neck," dip it in the broth to remove any sand and then into the melted butter. When all the clams are eaten, sip the delicious broth. Stop when you reach the sandy sediment. Serve Tuscan Bread with the steamers.

# chowders

The word *chowder* comes from the French word *chaudrée*, a fish soup with potatoes and bacon cooked in a *chaudron* (cauldron), a cast iron or copper soup pot.

The two most famous chowders are the New England and Manhattan clam chowders. New England clam chowder is very rich, with milk and cream, whereas Manhattan clam chowder is a vegetable soup with tomatoes and clam juice. Both are excellent. I make Manhattan chowder for family dinners, whereas New England chowder is more festive so I cook it for luncheons or serve it as a first course in a dinner party. I buy either littleneck or soft-shell clams (steamers). The soft-shell are generally steamed, but I love them in chowders.

# manhattan clam chowder

36 littleneck or soft-shell clams

4 cups water

1 (28-ounce) can peeled Italian plum tomatoes

6 ounces slab bacon, diced (about 2 cups)

3 small onions, peeled and chopped (1 1/2 cups)

1 small leek, white only, chopped (1/2 cup)

2 small Yukon Gold potatoes,
peeled and diced (1 1/2 cups)

1 green bell pepper,
seeded, quartered, and diced (1 cup)

1 celery stalk, sliced and diced (3/4 cup)

1 bay leaf

Few sprigs of fresh thyme
or 1 teaspoon dried thyme

Freshly ground black pepper

Salt

Soak the clams in cold salted water for 15 minutes. Scrub them clean with a wire brush under cold running water. Put the clams in a 9-quart heavy-bottomed soup pot with the water. Cover the pot and bring the water to a hard boil. The clams will open in 3 to 5 minutes, depending on their size. With tongs, remove them as they open to a plate. When cool, remove the clams from their shells (for the soft-shell clams, pull off and discard the black skin that covers the siphon, or neck) and chop them coarsely. Reserve.

Strain the clam juice; you should have about 5 cups. Reserve.

Drain the tomatoes and reserve the juices for another preparation (do not use the juices for the soup; it will dilute the clam juice). Chop the tomatoes (2 cups). Reserve.

In the same soup pot, over medium heat, fry the bacon until lightly brown, stirring all the while to prevent burning. Add the onions and leek and cook, stirring, for 5 minutes or until the onions and leek are wilted.

Add the chopped tomatoes. Stir and cover. Braise over low heat for 10 minutes, checking once in a while to make sure that nothing is burning. Add the potatoes, green pepper, celery, bay leaf, thyme, and clam juice. Bring to a boil, cover, reduce the heat, and simmer for 35 minutes.

Add the reserved chopped clams to the soup and cook without boiling for 1 minute, just enough to warm them through. Taste and correct seasoning with pepper and salt if necessary.

# new england clam chowder

New England chowder is a rich soup, perfect for a "champagne" luncheon in the winter followed by a tossed salad like the Haricots Verts with Wild Mushrooms (page 141) and a free-form apple tart (page 188) for dessert. Traditionally, the soup is made with milk and cream; use only milk if you want a lighter version.

24 littleneck or soft-shell clams

3 cups water

3 ounces bacon, cut into small pieces (about 1 cup)

1 large onion, peeled and diced (1 1/2 cups)

2 medium Russet potatoes, peeled and diced (1 1/2 cups)

1 cup milk (whole, 2%, or 1%)

1 cup heavy cream or half-and-half

1 tablespoon chopped fresh parsley

1 tablespoon chopped fresh chives

Croutons (page 161)

Salt

Soak the clams in cold salted water for 15 minutes, then scrub them clean with a wire brush under cold running water. Put the clams with the water in an 8-quart heavy-bottomed soup pot and cover. Bring the water to a hard boil. The clams will open in 3 to 5 minutes depending on their size. Check them and with tongs, remove them to a plate as they open. When cool, remove the clams from their shells (for soft-shell clams, pull off and discard the black skin that covers the siphon, or neck) and chop them coarsely. Reserve.

Boil down the cooking liquid to 2 cups and strain into a bowl. Reserve.

Wash and dry the soup pot, then fry the bacon until lightly brown. Stir in the onion and cook until the onion is wilted but not brown, about 5 to 10 minutes. Add the potatoes and cook for 5 minutes, stirring occasionally. Pour the reserved clam liquid over the vegetables and bacon. Cover the pot tightly and simmer gently for 20 minutes or until the potatoes are tender. Be careful that the liquid does not evaporate. Whisk the milk and the cream into the soup. Cool and reserve (can be done 2 to 3 hours ahead of time).

Just before serving, bring the soup just below the boil. Add the reserved clams and cook just long enough to heat them, but do not boil the liquid, which will toughen the clams. Taste and correct seasoning with salt if necessary.

Ladle the soup into individual soup bowls and sprinkle parsley and chives over the soup. Serve croutons on the side.

# portuguese cream of salt cod soup

You either like salt cod or you don't, so this soup is for salt cod lovers. According to fishmongers and lovers of salt cod, the fish is best when it is salted and dried on the fishing boats!

1 pound salt cod

1 pound Russet potatoes,
peeled and cut into ¹/₂-inch cubes (2 ¹/₂ cups)

1 medium onion,
quartered and stuck with 4 whole cloves

2 garlic cloves, peeled

Bouquet garni: 1 celery stalk, several sprigs
of flat-leaf parsley, sprigs of fresh thyme,
and bay leaf tied with a long string

2 ¹/₂ quarts water

¹/₂ cup heavy cream

Freshly ground black pepper

Salt

Croutons (page 161)

Place the cod in a large bowl of cold water. Soak overnight or for several hours under water flowing in a stream from the tap, desalting the cod. Drain the cod and cut it into small pieces (2 ¹/₂ cups).

In a 6-quart heavy-bottomed pot, combine the cod, potatoes, onion, garlic, and bouquet garni. Tie the string of the bouquet garni to one of the pot handles. Pour the water over the salt cod and vegetables. Bring to a boil, cover, reduce the heat, and simmer for 30 minutes. Cool for 10 minutes before the next step.

Purée the soup in a blender or food processor in several batches until smooth. Whisk in the cream. Season with pepper and salt if necessary.

Just before serving, reheat the soup and serve with croutons.

# youska
# a russian peasant potato
# and lox wings soup

This soup comes from my friend Harvey S. Shipley Miller's nannie, Rose, who was a Russian from Kiev. Any good Jewish "appetizing" store, such as Russ & Daughters or Zabar's in New York City, can supply lox wings (the head fins of mild cured salmon). Substitute fresh salmon if you do not care for the strong aroma of cured salmon.

2 pounds Yukon Gold potatoes, peeled and quartered (5 cups)

1 medium onion, coarsely chopped (1 cup)

1/2 pound carrots, peeled and cut into 2-inch-long pieces and quartered lengthwise

1 pound lox wings or fresh salmon

Bouquet garni (1 small bay leaf, 2 sprigs of fresh thyme, and 1/2 celery stalk)

Kosher salt

Sour cream

Butter

Toasted rye bread or pumpernickel, rubbed with a clove of garlic and buttered

Pasta such as tagliatelle (optional)

In a 9-quart heavy-bottomed pot, combine the potatoes, onion, carrots, lox wings, and salt. Add enough cold water to cover the ingredients by 2 inches. Add the bouquet garni, tying the string to the soup pot handle. Bring to a boil, cover, and simmer 30 minutes or until the potatoes are cooked and the carrots are al dente. If you plan to add pasta, put into the pot for the last 8 minutes of cooking.

On the table, have kosher salt, sour cream, butter, and the toasted bread to accompany the soup. Serve the soup very hot.

# meat
# +poultry
# soups

# 5

All the vegetable soups enriched with bacon are farm soups, with wonderful flavors and natural gelatin. It's traditional to kill pigs around Christmas and keep the belly to pickle or smoke. Today, in the States, you might need to go to a butcher who will cut a large slab of bacon, or you can substitute pancetta. Buy bacon that is not excessively smoked, otherwise you will need to blanch it to avoid a strong smoke taste in the soup. Do not trim the fat, nor the rind, which give flavor and body to the soups. The bacon poaches in the fat and will not render fat, as it does when fried. Trim the fat and rind when you are ready to serve.

I have always loved the chili I ate in Tulsa, Oklahoma, and I found a way to adapt it into a delicious beef soup for the winter holidays when I need to feed so many people.

All these soups, apart from the Chicken Breast Soup, mellow when they are made two or three days ahead.

# goulash soup

Here's a soup for a big crowd, served with spaetzle noodles. The noodles are easy to make, but if you don't have the inclination, substitute your favorite pasta.

4 pounds beef brisket or boneless chuck

1/2 cup vegetable oil

2 tablespoons butter

2 medium onions, chopped coarsely (2 cups)

1 large red bell pepper,
seeded and cut into small cubes (2 cups)

2 tablespoons mild paprika

1/2 teaspoon cayenne

4 garlic cloves, peeled and coarsely chopped

3 pounds tomatoes, peeled, seeded, and chopped,
or 2 (28-ounce) cans Italian plum tomatoes,
drained and chopped

2 large carrots,
cut into 1/2-inch-thick slices (1 1/2 cups)

Several sprigs of parsley

3 1/2 quarts Beef Broth (page 2),
Chicken Broth (page 3), or a commercial broth
or bouillon cubes

1/2 teaspoon red pepper flakes
tied in cheesecloth

1 tablespoon salt

Spaetzle (page 117)

2 tablespoons all-purpose flour

1 teaspoon paprika

3/4 cup heavy cream or sour cream

Freshly ground black pepper

Trim the meat and remove the gristle. Tie the trimmings and gristle in cheesecloth and reserve. Cut the meat into small cubes.

In a large nonstick skillet, heat 1/4 cup of the vegetable oil with the butter. Brown the meat in two batches, stirring occasionally, about 20 minutes in all. Transfer the meat to a 9-quart heavy-bottomed pot.

Add the remaining 1/4 cup vegetable oil to the skillet and brown the onions and red pepper, stirring for a minute. Add 1 1/2 table-spoons paprika (be sure it has not been in your spice cupboard too long) and the cayenne. Mix the spices thoroughly with the vegetables and continue browning for another 5 minutes without burning the onions. Add the garlic; stir for another minute or two and transfer to the soup pot.

Add the tomatoes, carrots, and parsley. Pour the broth over the meat and vegetables; bury the cheesecloth packages of meat trimmings and red pepper flakes. Add salt.

Bring to a boil, cover, reduce the heat, and simmer for 2 hours or until the meat is very tender.

Meanwhile, prepare the spaetzle.

In a medium bowl, mix the flour, 1/2 table-spoon paprika, a pinch of salt, and the cream. Pour it into the soup. Bring the goulash soup back to a boil. Taste and correct seasoning.

To serve, put several spaetzle in each soup plate or bowl and pour the goulash soup over them.

# spaetzle

You can make your own spaetzle without a special gadget, using just a knife and a wooden board or paddle. It looks kind of strange to pour a pancake-like batter on a board and cut it with the back of a knife, but it works. As soon as the batter hits the boiling water it cooks into these long free-form shreds like egg noodles—they are delicious with melted butter and parsley and great for soups.

2 large eggs

¾ cup water

⅛ teaspoon freshly grated nutmeg

½ teaspoon salt

Freshly ground black pepper

1 ½ cups all-purpose flour

3 tablespoons butter

2 tablespoons chopped parsley

In the bowl of a heavy-duty mixer, combine the eggs, water, nutmeg, salt, and pepper. Beat the mixture at medium speed, gradually adding the flour. The mixture should have the consistency of thick pancake batter. Set aside for 1 hour.

Bring 2 quarts of salted water to a boil in a large pan and place a large bowl of cold water next to the stove.

At first, to get the hang of it, ladle a small amount of the batter onto a paddle or a cutting board (if the batter spreads too fast, mix a bit more flour to the batter). Then, with the back of a 5-inch knife blade, cut a ¼-inch strip of batter (the batter should stick to the knife as it slides off the board into the boiling water). Repeat with all the batter on your board; it should look like egg drop soup. Spaetzle will have no shape or definition in the boiling water; once you transfer them to the cold water, they separate into thin strips.

Wait for the spaetzle to come back to the surface of the water and count 30 seconds. With a large-mesh ladle, drain and put in cold water to stop the cooking. Repeat the procedure until all batter is cooked into spaetzles.

When ready to eat, drain the spaetzle into a large nonstick skillet, add the butter and parsley, and sprinkle with salt and pepper. Heat on medium-high heat until the spaetzle are warmed through.

# escarole and meat ball soup

You can feed a large crowd of family or guests with this delicious soup. It's an expandable soup for the holidays; add more meat balls and broth when more people are coming for dinner. This is several courses in one pot, with pasta, meat, salad, and cheese!

**For the Meat Balls:**

1 pound lean ground beef

1/2 cup bread crumbs

1 garlic clove, mashed to a paste

1 tablespoon minced parsley

1 tablespoon minced fresh thyme or basil

1/4 cup grated Parmesan cheese

1 egg

1/2 teaspoon salt

Freshly ground black pepper

1 tablespoon olive oil

**For the Escarole Soup:**

10 loose cups escarole leaves, washed

Salt

2 quarts Beef Broth (page 2), Chicken Broth (page 3), or a commercial broth or bouillon cubes

1/2 cup orzo or broken vermicelli

A bowl of grated Romano or Parmesan cheese

Preheat the oven to 300 degrees.

**The meat balls:** In a large mixing bowl, combine the meat ball ingredients and mix well. Roll the mixture into 1 to 1 1/2-inch balls. Bake the meatballs for 5 minutes in a pan greased with olive oil. Reserve for later. (If you don't want to put all the meat balls in the soup, freeze the remaining ones for another soup.)

**The soup:** Place the escarole in a large pan and sprinkle with 1/4 teaspoon salt. There should be enough water clinging to the leaves to cook with. Cover and slowly bring the escarole to a boil. When wilted, drain the escarole and reserve.

In a 6-quart pot, combine the broth, escarole, meatballs, and 2 teaspoons salt. Bring to a boil, cover, reduce the heat, and simmer for 30 minutes.

Five minutes before serving, bring the soup to a boil and add the orzo or vermicelli. Serve with grated cheese on the side.

# scotch broth

It's more than a broth, it's a complete meal. Although traditionally a "winter warmer" soup, the vegetables can be mixed, matched, and changed according to the season. For example, the traditional winter vegetables: carrots, celery, onions, and turnips can be changed to zucchini, tomatoes, and eggplant during the summer.

For the lamb, choose either shanks, neck, or shoulder, but if you cannot find these cuts of meat, buy the shank part of a leg and ask the butcher to cut it into slices with the bones, which enrich the broth. In Scotland, the soup is cooked in water and the meat is not browned. This is my version:

4 pounds lamb shanks or lamb shoulder,
cut into thick slices

2 tablespoons olive oil

2 teaspoons sugar

1 tablespoon salt

2½ quarts Chicken Broth (page 3),
or a commercial broth or bouillon cubes

4 tablespoons pearl barley, rinsed

1 small savoy cabbage (about 2 pounds)

2 carrots, peeled and chopped (1 cup)

1 large leek, white only, chopped (2 cups)

2 pounds Yukon Gold potatoes,
Fingerlings or Creamers, peeled

½ cup chopped parsley or basil

Trim the fat from the meat, if any, and discard. Heat 2 tablespoons oil in a large skillet; saute the meat in two batches, sprinkling the sugar and about 1 teaspoon salt over it. When the meat is lightly caramelized, transfer to a 9-quart heavy-bottomed pot. Pour the broth over it. Over medium heat, bring the broth to just under a boil and skim the fat and scum off the top. Add the barley, 2 teaspoons salt (my homemade broth is very lightly salted but be careful with salt using commercial broth). Cover the pot, simmer for 1 hour.

Meanwhile, discard the tough dark-green cabbage leaves; quarter the cabbage and cut out and discard the stalk. Cut the cabbage into thin slices. Yields about 8 cups.

Add the cabbage, carrots, and leek to the soup pot, pushing down so the cabbage is submerged. Cover and cook another 30 minutes. Can be prepared to this step ahead of time.

Add the potatoes on top of the cabbage. Cover and cook for another 30 minutes or until the potatoes are tender.

With tongs, remove the meat and bone it, discard the bones. Put the meat back in the soup pot. Reheat and, just before serving, mix in the herbs, either parsley or basil.

# ike's chili-bean soup

Ike's Chili Parlor was famous in Tulsa, Oklahoma, where my husband grew up. Wayne's sister would bring us pots of chili when she visited us in New York, and finally Wayne was able to reproduce chili, just like the one he ate at Ike's. Today, I make it into a very rich soup. The secret to the richness of this chili is the beef suet, which you must order from a butcher. The soup can be made ahead of time.

**For the Beans:**

6 cups parboiled red beans (see page 78)

1 medium onion,
peeled and stuck with 2 whole cloves

1 large carrot, peeled and cut in half

1 garlic clove, peeled

2 celery stalks with leaves,
cut into 2-inch pieces (1 cup)

6 cups Beef Broth (page 2), or a commercial broth or bouillon cubes

1–2 teaspoons salt

Freshly ground black pepper

**For the Chili:**

3 1/2 pounds beef brisket or boneless chuck

6 ounces beef suet, cut into 3/4-inch cubes

1/2 cup water

3 garlic cloves, minced

2 tablespoons Chili Powder (page 121)
or 4 tablespoons commercial chili powder

1 tablespoon ground cumin

1 tablespoon dried oregano

1 1/2 teaspoons hot paprika

2 cups Beef Broth (page 2), or a commercial broth or bouillon cubes

Salt

2 tablespoons masa harina

1/2 cup water

**The beans:** In a 9-quart heavy-bottomed pot, combine the beans, onion, carrot, garlic, celery, and broth. Bring to a boil, reduce the heat, cover, and simmer 1 1/2 hours or until the beans are cooked. Add salt toward the end of cooking.

When the beans are cooked, scoop out 2 1/2 cups of beans and 2 cups of bean broth and purée in a blender or food processor until smooth. Set aside.

**The chili:** Trim the beef of fat and gristle. Cut into 1-inch cubes. By hand, cut each cube into very thin, small pieces. (It takes time.) Or, if using a food processor, just freeze the meat for 20 minutes. Use the metal blade to chop the meat in at least six batches, turning the machine on and off eight to ten times or until coarsely chopped.

Put the suet in a 4-quart pot with the water and cook over moderately high heat, watching it carefully for 15 minutes. Strain the rendered suet into another soup pot for the chili and discard the solids.

Reheat the rendered suet and add the chopped meat. Cook, stirring, over moderate heat, until the meat loses its red color, about 10 minutes. Do not let the meat brown.

Add the garlic, half the chili powder, the cumin, oregano, paprika, and broth. Bring to a boil, reduce the heat, cover, and simmer for 1 1/2 hours, about the same time it takes to cook the beans. Taste and adjust seasoning with salt and more spices.

Combine the bean purée and the remaining beans with their broth with the chili meat. Reheat; taste and correct seasoning. Keep warm.

Bring to a boil the remaining chili powder and 1 1/2 cups of water in a 2-quart saucepan; reduce the heat and simmer for 15 minutes. In a small bowl, mix the masa harina with the water, 1 teaspoon at a time for a moderately thick paste. Whisk the masa harina mixture into the hot sauce. Serve on the side with the soup.

*makes about ¾ cup*

# chili powder

Guajillo and japones are dried chiles. Take care not to inhale the fumes when you grind them because they are very strong. Do not rub your eyes.

2 ounces guajillo chiles
.................................................................
1 ounce japones chiles
.................................................................

Toast the peppers in a nonstick skillet over low heat for a few minutes until they darken. Remove and discard the stems, and break the chiles into small pieces. Grind them with their seeds in an electric coffee or spice mill or in an electric blender until they are reduced to a fine powder. Keep in a plastic container for several months.

# spanish chickpea and pork soup

Josephina is an Andalusian, wife of Paco, who did a lot of construction work in our house. I had absolutely no luck cooking chickpeas until I met her; the peas were always hard as rocks even after several hours of cooking. According to Josephina, only Spanish chickpeas are worth eating! As I told her I could not go to Spain every time I wanted to make her soup, that I had to buy them locally. I learned to soak the peas overnight in salted boiling water. That's Josephina's way and it works.

4 cups dried chickpeas

4 tablespoons salt

**For the Meats:**

2-pound slab of lightly smoked bacon

3 pounds spare ribs

2 pounds fresh ham in a large slice with the rind

¼ pound salted pork

**For the Vegetables:**

2 pounds Yukon Gold potatoes

1 pound Swiss chard

1 tablespoon salt or more

Freshly ground pepper

Horseradish

Mustard

In a large bowl, cover the chickpeas with about 4 quarts of boiling water and add the salt. (Don't worry at the amount of salt—the chickpeas are rinsed after soaking.) Soak overnight.

Drain and wash off the chickpeas under running cold water.

**The meats:** In a saucepan, cover the bacon with water. Bring to a boil and boil for 5 minutes or so; drain and refresh under running cold water.

In a 9-quart heavy-bottomed pot, combine the chickpeas and the meats. Cover with about 5 quarts of hot water from the tap. Bring to a boil slowly, skimming the top as scum starts to gather on top.

**The vegetables:** Peel and cut the potatoes into large cubes. Remove the leaves of the Swiss chard and reserve for another preparation, such as Swiss Chard, Potato, and Carrot Soup (page 31). Peel the ribs of the Swiss chard and cut them into 2-inch sticks. Add the vegetables to the boiling soup and sprinkle with salt and pepper. Bring again to a boil for 30 minutes; reduce the heat, cover, and simmer at a gentle boil for another 2 hours, skimming once in a while; add salt and freshly ground pepper to taste. As the soup cooks, the liquid takes on a milky sheen.

Remove the meat and cut it into pieces. Serve the broth with the vegetables, then more broth with the meat for a second serving. Have several condiments on the side—horseradish, mustard, etc.—to season the meat.

# sausage, chickpea, and potato soup

The essence of this soup is Italian, and it's very tasty. Dried chickpeas must be soaked overnight before cooking: 1 cup dried chickpeas makes 2 1/2 cups soaked.

1 cup dried chickpeas
or 1 pound cooked chickpeas (see page 78)

Salt

1/2 pound fresh Italian sausage

1 tablespoon fresh rosemary leaves, minced

3 garlic cloves, peeled and smashed

4 tablespoons olive oil, plus more for dribbling

1 small onion, peeled and sliced (1/2 cup)

1/3 teaspoon red pepper flakes

1 (14-ounce) can crushed Italian plum tomatoes

3/4 pound Russet potatoes,
peeled and cut into 1/2-inch cubes

6 cups Chicken Broth (page 3), or a commercial broth or bouillon cubes

Toasts of Tuscan Bread (page 158),
rubbed with raw garlic

If you are using dried chickpeas, bring water to a boil in a 4-quart pot and pour it over the chickpeas and 1 tablespoon salt (the salt is very important, helping the peas to soften). Soak overnight. Drain and pour boiling water over them. Cover and cook for 45 minutes or until tender.

Remove the casing of the sausage and crumble the sausage with the rosemary and one garlic clove. Heat 1 tablespoon of the oil in a 6-quart heavy-bottomed pot and add the crumbled sausage with the garlic clove. Sauté for a few minutes, stirring all the while. Transfer the sausage to a plate and discard the garlic.

Heat the remaining 3 tablespoons olive oil in the pot. Add the onion and the last two crushed garlic cloves and the red pepper flakes; stir for 5 minutes occasionally. When the onion turns a rich tawny color, stir in the tomatoes. Cover, reduce the heat, and simmer for 10 minutes, stirring once in a while. Add the chickpeas, potatoes, and the reserved sausage; sprinkle with 2 teaspoons salt. Pour the broth in the pot and bring to a boil. Cover, reduce the heat, and cook at a gentle boil 40 minutes or until the potatoes are very tender.

**VARIATION:** If desired, mash several potato cubes in the soup to thicken the soup. Taste and correct the seasoning before serving. Place a toast rubbed with garlic in each soup plate; pour the soup over the bread and dribble olive oil on top of the soup.

# spelt soup

Spelt is an old-fashioned wheat cereal found in health food stores and even in super-markets. It is loved in Provence, where there are as many recipes for *soupe d'épeautre* as there are cooks.

Salt pork in France is called *petit salé,* a lightly salted fresh bacon; in the States, I buy pancetta or lean bacon. The soup can be prepared ahead of time but will thicken while it waits. Have on hand some broth to thin it before serving.

1 pound bacon or pancetta

1 1/2 cups spelt

1 1/2 cups parboiled navy or cannellini beans (see page 78)

1 white of leek, chopped (1 cup)

1 medium onion, peeled and chopped (1 cup)

2 large garlic cloves, peeled

1 teaspoon salt

3 quarts water

Cover the bacon or pancetta with cold water in a 4-quart pan. Bring to a boil and boil for 10 minutes. Drain and rinse the meat under cold running water.

Wash the spelt under running cold water.

In a 6-quart heavy-bottomed pot, combine the meat, spelt, beans, onion, and garlic; sprinkle with the salt. Pour the water into the soup pot. Cover and slowly bring to a boil over low to medium heat. Cook just under the boil for 3 hours.

Remove the meat with tongs, trim the fat, and cut meat into 1-inch cubes. Reheat the soup with the cut-up meat. Taste and correct the seasoning.

# kohlrabi soup

This is a typical peasant soup for the autumn, when the kohlrabi is young. It is made with water and flavored with bacon; in France, as in other parts of Europe, lightly salted fresh bacon is the typical cut of pork used in soups. In the States, I substitute pancetta or slab bacon, parboiled. A kohlrabi is a cross between a cabbage and a turnip. Choose small kohlrabi, the size of tennis balls; they are more tender than the huge ones.

2 ½ pounds kohlrabi

1 medium Russet potato,
peeled and quartered (1 cup)

1 ½ pounds pancetta or slab bacon, parboiled

8 cups water

Salt

Freshly ground black pepper

Cut off the shoots that stick out of the kohlrabi and discard. Peel the kohlrabi with a vegetable peeler. Cut into ½-inch cubes (6 cups).

Put the kohlrabi, potato, pork, and water in an 6-quart heavy-bottomed pot; bring to a boil, cover, reduce the heat, and simmer gently for 1 hour or until the kohlrabi is tender.

With tongs, transfer the pork to a board, trim the fat, and cut the meat into large cubes. Reserve. In several batches, purée the soup with some of the broth in a blender or use an immersion blender. Transfer the pork back to the soup.

Just before dinner, reheat the soup. Taste and correct seasoning with salt and pepper.

# german lentil soup

You can make this soup a day ahead of time. I find it mellows spending a night in the refrigerator.

2 tablespoons lard or olive oil

4 lamb chops

1 large onion, coarsely chopped (1 cup)

2 carrots, cut into ¼-inch cubes (1 ½ cups)

1 celery stalk, cut into ¼-inch cubes (½ cup)

1 pound Russet potatoes, cut into ¼-inch cubes, or 2 large red peppers, cored and cut into ¼-inch cubes

4 garlic cloves, peeled and coarsely chopped

1 (28-ounce) can crushed Italian plum tomatoes

1 pound lentils

10 sprigs of parsley

2 ½ quarts Chicken Broth (page 3), or a commercial broth or bouillon cubes

Sea salt

Freshly ground black pepper

In a 9-quart pot, heat the olive oil or the lard and sauté the lamb chops over medium heat for 15 minutes, stirring occasionally.

Transfer the meat to a plate and add the onion, carrots, celery, potatoes or red peppers, and garlic to the pot. Stir the vegetables, cover, reduce the heat, and braise for 5 minutes.

Add the crushed tomatoes, lentils, the meat, the parsley, and broth; sprinkle with salt and pepper. Bring to a boil, cover, reduce the heat, and simmer for 1 hour. Taste and adjust seasoning. Bone the chops and cut meat into pieces; discard the bones.

Reheat when ready to serve.

# chicken breast soup with mussels

Chicken marries well with shellfish, especially mussels. You can substitute clams if you prefer.

1 whole chicken breast, cut into halves

1/4 cup olive oil

2 medium carrots,
peeled and cut in 1/2-inch-thick slices (1 1/2 cups)

1 medium white turnip, peeled, split in half, and cut crosswise into 1/2-inch pieces (1/2 cup)

2 cups Chicken Broth or more (page 3),
Vegetable Broth (page 5), or a commercial broth or bouillon cubes

Salt

1 small zucchini, ends trimmed, split in half and cut crosswise into 1/2-inch pieces (1 cup)

2 pounds mussels (or clams)

2 large shallots, peeled and coarsely chopped

1/2 cup water

1/2 cup white wine, such as Chardonnay

A large pinch of saffron strands

1/2 cup heavy cream or half-and-half

Preheat the oven to 350 degrees.

Place the chicken breast, skin side up, in a small oiled roasting pan. Bake in the oven for 20 minutes, basting occasionally with 2 to 3 tablespoons water. Drain and set aside.

In a large nonstick skillet, heat 2 tablespoons of the oil. Add the carrots, turnip, and 1/2 cup of the broth. Sprinkle with salt. Cover, reduce the heat, and braise for 10 minutes or until the vegetables are tender; if the vegetables get dry, add more broth. Add the zucchini to the skillet and cook another 5 minutes or so.

Meanwhile, scrub the mussels clean with a wire brush under cold running water and put them in a 6-quart heavy-bottomed pot. Add the shallots, remaining 2 tablespoons olive oil, the water, and the white wine. Cover and cook over high heat, shaking the pot until the mussels open, 2 to 3 minutes.

Strain the mussel liquor through a double thickness of cheesecloth; you should have about 2 cups. Shell the mussels and combine the mussel liquor, remaining broth, saffron, and cream with the mussels and vegetables and reheat in the same pot. Taste and adjust the seasoning.

Bone and skin the chicken; cut the meat on a slant into 1/4-inch-thick slices on a cutting board. Garnish each preheated plate with chicken pieces and pour the broth over it with the mussels and vegetables. Garnish with strands of saffron.

# mexican chicken soup with tortilla chips

Friends of Susan Friedland, my editor, raved about a Mexican soup of chicken, chicken broth, and lime juice, served with tortillas. One summer night, I invited a group of friends to taste my own Mexican soup, followed with a salad and a soup of a light custard with ice cream and prunes (see page 179). The menu worked beautifully, especially because the labor can be done ahead of time.

6 chicken thighs and drumsticks or 2 whole chicken breasts, split in half and not boned

1/4 cup fresh lime juice

4 tablespoons olive oil

1 tablespoon mashed garlic

1 teaspoon salt

6 cups Mexican Chicken Broth (page 130)

1 cup thinly sliced scallions

Up to 1/3 cup lime juice

Salt

Tortilla Chips (see page 163) or store-bought

5 ounces queso fresco or feta cheese, crumbled (1 1/2 cups)

Place the chicken pieces flat in a large 3-quart glass baking dish. Drizzle the lime juice, olive oil, garlic, and salt over the chicken, cover, and refrigerate overnight.

Bring the chicken to room temperature before barbecuing. Light a fire in your barbecue.

Put the chicken directly over the coals to brown. Turn after 3 to 5 minutes or so to avoid burning, again 3 to 5 minutes on the other side. When all the pieces are browned, move them away from the coals and cover with the barbecue lid. Cook for 15 minutes for the thighs or drumsticks or 10 minutes for the chicken breast; turn the pieces over and cook for 10 more minutes for the thighs and drumsticks. During the cooking, baste with the marinade of lime juice and oil. The breasts should be removed earlier in order not to dry out the white meat. Reserve, covered.

Bone and skin the chicken and cut into serving size. Add the chicken pieces to the broth, along with the scallions and lime juice (start with 1/4 cup lime juice and add more to taste). Sprinkle with salt if necessary. Refrigerate only if you make the soup several hours ahead of time.

When ready to eat, reheat the soup.

To serve, place Tortilla Chips in each soup plate and ladle the chicken soup over them. Pass a bowl of crumbled cheese.

# mexican chicken broth

Marguerite Casparian, who is married to an Episcopalian priest, has lived all over the world. Right now she lives in Florence, but for many years she and her husband lived in Mexico. She learned to make this delicious chicken broth there: "I learned to make homemade broth from my grandmother and some secrets about seasoning from a guy who was tarring the roof on the house where we were staying in Mexico. I was looking for herbs, and he came down to ask what I was making. When I told him chicken soup he said I didn't need the handful I'd gathered—just thyme and mint. So this is a Mexican chicken broth made with my grandmother's patience and a roofer's taste buds."

4 tablespoons olive oil

1 large onion, peeled and chopped (1 ½ cups)

1 small carrot, sliced (½ cup)

1 large celery stalk,
cleaned and sliced (1 ½ cups)

3 large garlic cloves, peeled

Several sprigs of parsley, chopped

1 (4-pound) chicken

2 large sprigs fresh mint
or 1 ½ teaspoons dried mint

2 large sprigs fresh thyme
or 1 ½ teaspoons dried thyme

4 quarts water

1 tablespoon salt

1 tablespoon black peppercorns

2 large peeled tomatoes, chopped, or 1 (14-ounce) can of Italian plum tomatoes, drained and chopped

In a 9-quart heavy-bottomed pot, heat 2 tablespoons of the olive oil over medium heat. Stir in the onion, carrot, celery, 1 garlic clove, and the parsley. Cook for 10 minutes, stirring occasionally.

Add the chicken, mint, and thyme. Pour in the water, sprinkle with the salt, and add the peppercorns. Bring slowly to a boil. Cover partially, reduce the heat, and simmer for 3 hours. With a long-handled spoon, occasionally skim the fat that rises to the surface.

Meanwhile, heat the remaining 2 tablespoons olive oil in a large skillet. Add the chopped tomatoes and 1 garlic clove. Sauté over high heat, stirring all the while for 3 minutes. Purée the tomato and garlic in a food processor and reserve for later.

Gently scoop out the chicken and let it drain in a sieve placed over a bowl. Bone the chicken, discard the bones and skin, and cut the meat in serving pieces and refrigerate for sandwiches.

Strain the broth, discarding the vegetables and peppercorns, and add the reserved tomato mixture. Reheat the broth and taste for seasoning (2 quarts). If you have more liquid, boil it down to 2 quarts to concentrate the flavors.

When cool, refrigerate the broth or freeze it. If you refrigerate it, remember to use it within three days or reboil it to avoid spoilage.

# salads

## ON VINAIGRETTE

A well-seasoned salad is de rigueur; sometimes I eat salads with very fresh ingredients that taste blah simply because the dressing (the core that brings all the ingredients together) is either bland, made with so-so vinegar or so-so oil, or there's too much or too little dressing. When preparing the salad greens, I tear the large lettuce leaves with my hands, never with a knife—a knife bruises the delicate leaves—and I keep the small leaves intact.

I love to boast about my vinaigrette. I make it with my husband's vinegar and with olive oil from Nyons, the renowned olive town in the Drôme Provençale where I live now. Wayne's vinegar is the main reason I live in Provence instead of New York City, where I had a cooking school, A La Bonne Cocotte, for thirty years.

In the early years of my school, back in the seventies, Wayne was the wine buyer for the classes. My wine budget was severely limited, and it was Wayne's job to find a cheap, drinkable wine. He found José Garcia Spanish wine for 99 cents a bottle and bought ten cases!

One day, Wayne reached for a bottle and found its neck broken. He started to pour the wine into the sink when the aroma caught his attention: it was no longer wine but the fresh scent of vinegar, made without the help of a "mother." From then on, Wayne was our supplier of vinegar.

**6**

We started to make vinegar, using a small wine barrel, adding some José Garcia "mother" and filling it up with wine. But soon, all our friends and students wanted Wayne's vinegar. Joseph Swann, the wine maker of Zinfandel par excellence in the 1970s, sent us an old thirty-gallon wooden barrel by Greyhound bus and Wayne was in business.

After winning a blind vinegar testing, Wayne became impossible: the idea of making vinegar for just our friends was not enough—he had to get into large-scale commercial production. I was not too happy about that until he talked about buying a barn in Provence, in the Côtes du Rhône area where he could buy bulk wine cheap.

That caught my attention; besides cooking, my other passion is real estate. From an initial search for a barn, we ended up buying the remains of a medieval chateau in the town of Nyons, where we live today.

Wayne continues making vinegar for friends, his dreams of becoming a vinegar baron long forgotten. Here, in his own words, is Wayne's method.

"Making vinegar is dead easy because the bacteria do the real work. Wine is made from grape juice by yeast that turn the sugar in the grape juice into alcohol. Once this is done, bacteria take over and turn the alcohol into acetic acid, making vinegar. You do have to be careful that the wine is not overloaded with chemicals that will kill the bugs. This happened to me once and I nearly panicked thinking my barrel had gone bad. Lydie suggested dumping out that batch and trying somewhat better wine, which I did—it worked out fine.

"Keep the container with the wine in a relatively warm place, 75 degrees or so. If it's too cool, the bugs don't do their job and you wind up with wine from which all the alcohol has evaporated, but no vinegar. If it happens, just start over.

"You can make vinegar in almost any container. I've had good results using a half-gallon apple juice jar. Fill it almost full, but leave enough room at the top to have a large surface for the bacteria to get started. You don't need a "mother" to make vinegar. The bugs are all around us all the time and will find their home all by themselves. Cover the top with cheesecloth so air can get through.

"After a week or so, a white film will form on the surface; that's the "mother"; do not shake or stir—just leave it alone and let it work for you. You can start with just a little wine in the container and add the ends of bottles. Allow about three months after the final addition of wine for the vinegar to be finished, then bottle it and cork it. You can keep it for months or years, even. A friend in California has some of my vinegar from fifteen years ago that is still good. If you can find an oak barrel that has been used for wine or brandy, you can expect better results, but beware of using a brand-new one. They usually have a lot of sap still in the wood, which will ruin the first few batches."

# vinaigrette dressing with yogurt

Of course, we buy local olive oil because Nyons is a center of olive oil making here in northern Provence. The olive oil is made from one variety of olive called La Tanche; its delicate flavor makes it perfect for seasoning. In this dressing we cut down on the oil, adding yogurt to make the dressing less high in calories. The yogurt also keeps the dressing emulsified so successfully that often someone will ask if there is an egg yolk in the mixture. Here is a recipe for one cup of dressing, which is too much for any of the following salad recipes. I make more than I need and put it in a screw-top jar and refrigerate it. I have left the dressing in the refrigerator for no more than a week, but we do eat lots of salads with our soups.

Large pinch of salt

Freshly ground black pepper

1 large garlic clove

1 teaspoon mustard, Dijon type

3 tablespoons red wine vinegar

½ cup olive oil

4 tablespoons plain yogurt

Put the salt and pepper in a mixing bowl. Mash the garlic clove either with a garlic press or by rubbing it across the ends of the tines of a fork held against the bottom of the bowl. Add the mustard and vinegar, whisking thoroughly. Very slowly, whisk in the oil.

Whisk in the yogurt for a very creamy mixture. Taste and correct seasoning.

**NOTE:** When making a salad with greens, never toss the dressing with the greens ahead of time; the greens get soggy. Most often, I prepare salads ahead of time by putting the dressing in the bowl first, then placing the tossing set of fork and spoon crossways in the bowl, and finally adding the salad greens. The greens are protected by the fork and spoon from touching the dressing.

# wayne marshall's tossed salad

My husband, Wayne, frequently makes soups and salads with the leftovers from my classes. He is very proud of his salads, especially after the late Richard Olney, a talented but demanding cook and cookbook author, complimented him on a salad he had made with leftover duck.

It's impossible to give exact amounts of each ingredient; vary the ingredients and amounts to suit your taste and the number of people you are serving (and, of course, the amount of leftovers you have).

Sliced cooked meat (beef, lamb, or pork), cut into 1/2-inch-wide strips, or sliced cooked fowl (chicken, turkey, or duck), cut into 1/2-inch cubes

Olive oil

Cooked and peeled potatoes, thickly sliced

Chicory, torn into pieces

Watercress, coarse stems removed

Alfalfa sprouts

Jerusalem artichokes (uncooked), pared and thickly sliced

Pepperoncini salad peppers, drained

1/3 cup Vinaigrette Dressing or more (page 135)

Salt

Freshly ground black pepper

In a large skillet, quickly brown the meat in a little olive oil until it is crisp; remove and set aside in a mixing bowl.

Heat the potatoes in the same skillet, adding a little more oil if necessary, until they are slightly browned.

Toss the meat and potatoes with the chicory, watercress, sprouts, Jerusalem artichokes, and salad peppers in a large serving bowl.

Toss the Vinaigrette Dressing with the salad ingredients. Taste and correct seasoning, adding more dressing if necessary. Serve at once.

# colette valentin's chestnut salad

Colette Valentin, my neighbor, makes soups and salads very often for her fall and winter suppers. In the fall she cooks fresh chestnuts, which she combines with the wild mushrooms picked by her husband, Dédé. She uses oakleaf lettuce, lambs' tongue (*mâche*), or the light green leaves of chicory to produce a really interesting salad to follow a soup like the Jerusalem Artichoke Soup (page 28) or the Pumpkin Soup (page 34).

1 pound chestnuts

3 leaves of fresh sage or 1/2 teaspoon dried sage

1/2 pound portabello or chanterelle mushrooms, cleaned and cut into wedges

2 tablespoons olive oil

1/2 teaspoon sea salt

8 cups shredded salad greens, washed, spin-dried, and torn into pieces

1/2 cup Vinaigrette Dressing (page 135)

With a very sharp paring knife, peel the chestnuts, removing the tough outer shell and some of the second layer of skin.

In a 4-quart pan, cover the chestnuts and several sage leaves with a large amount of water. Bring to a boil, cover, reduce the heat, and simmer for 15 minutes or until the chestnuts can easily be pierced with the blade of a knife. Drain and peel the remaining skin while the chestnuts are still hot.

In a large nonstick pan, toss the mushrooms with the olive oil and salt over high heat, stir-frying for 2 minutes or until the mushrooms start to color.

In a large salad bowl, toss the greens, chestnuts, and mushrooms in the Vinaigrette Dressing. Taste and correct seasoning before serving immediately.

# chickpea salad

I make this salad very often during the winter because it can be kept in the refrigerator for several days—the more the chickpeas marinate in the dressing, the better the salad is. You need to bring it to room temperature before dinnertime. I serve the salad on a bed of crisp greens with several winter soups, like Celery Root Soup with Stilton (page 38) and the Butternut Soup with Cumin (page 33)

1 cup dried chickpeas or 2 cups canned chickpeas

1 tablespoon salt

2 garlic cloves, peeled and mashed to a paste

1 large shallot, peeled and
very thinly sliced (1/4 cup)

1/3 cup Vinaigrette Dressing (page 135)

8 cups loosely packed oakleaf salad greens,
washed and spun-dry

The night before you plan to serve, boil a large amount of water. Sprinkle 1 tablespoon salt over the chickpeas and cover with boiling water in a large mixing bowl.

Drain the chickpeas and put them in a 4-quart pan with a large amount of boiling water. Bring to a boil, cover, reduce the heat, and simmer for 35 minutes or until the chickpeas are tender, adding more water if the level falls below the beans. Depending on their age, the chickpeas should be done in 30 to 60 minutes.

Drain the chickpeas. Toss them with the garlic, shallot, and 1/4 cup of the dressing in a bowl. Taste for seasoning, adding perhaps a bit more vinegar or oil. Can be made a day or two ahead of time.

To serve, bring the chickpeas back to room temperature. In a salad bowl, add the remaining dressing and toss in the salad greens. Garnish a platter with the greens and add the chickpeas in the center of the greens.

# chicory salad with bacon, croutons, and poached eggs

France has two types of family restaurants: the *bistro,* which has an intimate feel, and the *brasserie,* a huge restaurant like a beer hall. This *salade frisée aux lardons* belongs to the brasserie type. Make it with the heart of a chicory salad head, picking out the white and the light green leaves, or buy a green called California frisée, found in upscale green markets now. I serve this salad year-round with soups such as Onion Soup (page 18), the Cold Summer Squash Soup (page 62), or the La Mouclade, a mussel soup (page 103).

8 cups loosely packed chicory salad or frissé

8 ounces slab of lean bacon or pancetta

1 cup Croutons (page 161)

1/3 cup Vinaigrette Dressing (page 135)

4 eggs

1 teaspoon white vinegar

Pick out the white and light green leaves of the chicory, then cut them into small pieces, or use the whole head of frisée. It should fill the spin-dry basket very loosely.

Slice off the rind of the bacon and discard. Dice the bacon. In a large nonstick skillet, cook the bacon until lightly brown (1 cup). Drain.

In a large bowl, toss the greens, bacon, and croutons in the vinaigrette dressing. Taste and correct seasoning.

Place the tossed salad on four individual plates.

Poach the eggs. Pour water and a dash of vinegar in one large or two medium skillets. Bring the water to a boil, break the eggs into the boiling water, and with a spatula, bring the white of each egg back on top of the yolk. As soon as the white turns milky color (less than 2 minutes), scoop the eggs out of the water with a fine-meshed sieve. Place one egg on top of each salad and serve immediately.

**NOTE:** To eat, break the runny yolk into the salad.

# couscous salad

This couscous salad originates in Algeria. When I have a crowd of vegetarians for supper, I serve a soup like Potage Crecy (page 12), made with water or vegetable broth, followed by this salad and a dessert of crepes (see page 182). Prepare the salad ahead of time; it develops flavor while waiting.

1 pound medium to coarse couscous

1 cup water

1/4 cup olive oil

3 medium tomatoes, seeded and cubed (3 cups)

2 cups fresh shelled peas or frozen green peas

4 ears fresh corn or 2 cups frozen corn

2 large grapefruits

1/2 cup Vinaigrette Dressing (page 135)

3 tablespoons minced scallions

Several small pepperoncini—small green peppers in brine—chopped

Sea salt

Freshly ground black pepper

Spread the couscous in a large pan. Boil the water with the olive oil. Pour over the couscous and with a fork, mix the couscous to absorb the liquid. Let stand for 20 minutes or so.

Place the cut-up tomatoes in a strainer to drain. Put the peas in a 3-quart pan with about 1/2 cup water. Bring to a boil and cook 5 minutes or until tender. Drain and reserve. For fresh corn, bring about 3 quarts of water to a boil and add the corn; cook until tender. Cut off the kernels with a knife and reserve. Or cook the frozen peas and the frozen corn according to the instructions on the packages and reserve.

With a serrated knife, peel the grapefruits, going into the flesh to remove the bitter white pith. Slip a sharp knife between the wedges and remove the grapefruit flesh.

Rub the couscous between your hands to fluff it. Transfer to a strainer lined with cheesecloth with a large overhang, placed over a pot of boiling water (or use a *couscoussier*). Cover the couscous with the overhang cheesecloth and place a lid over it and steam for 30 minutes.

In a large serving bowl, toss the couscous in the vinaigrette, along with the tomatoes, peas, corn, tomatoes, grapefruit wedges, scallions, and salad green peppers. Sprinkle with salt and pepper to taste and toss once more.

You can prepare the salad in the afternoon and leave it at room temperature for dinner or refrigerate it if it is prepared a day ahead of time.

# haricots verts with wild mushroom salad

When the first wild mushrooms appear in my market, I quickly put this salad on the menu; domestic mushrooms such as shiitake and portabellos are a good substitute. Try to buy the green beans, *haricots verts,* as soon as they appear at your market. The fresher they are, the better. If you can't find *haricots verts,* pick the thinnest green beans available. This salad goes well with Chicken Breast Soup with Mussels (page 128).

$^1/_2$ pound mushrooms

1 pound small green beans or haricots verts, trimmed

$^1/_4$ cup Vinaigrette Dressing (page 135)

Sea salt

Freshly ground black pepper

2 tablespoons olive oil

1 tablespoon fresh thyme leaves

Place the vinaigrette in a large serving bowl. Set aside.

Clean the mushrooms with a damp cloth. Trim and discard any tough stems. Quarter or cut the mushrooms into eighths, depending on their size. Set aside.

In a 4-quart saucepan, bring a large amount of water to a hard boil. Plunge the *haricots verts* into the boiling water. Count 2 minutes after the water comes back to the boil and taste one for doneness. Boil the haricots verts until just cooked through but still crisp. Drain them very well and quickly toss them in the dressing. Sprinkle with salt and pepper and toss once more. Set aside.

In a large nonstick skillet, heat the olive oil over medium-high heat. Raise the heat to high and stir-fry the mushrooms with the thyme for 4 minutes or until they start to color and lose their raw aspect. Sprinkle with salt and pepper and toss with the *haricots verts*. Taste and correct seasoning and serve immediately, before the salad becomes limp.

# goat cheese fritters on a bed of arugula and watercress

Choose a goat cheese (*chèvre*) that is firm to the touch. Blue cheese, Roquefort, and feta are good substitutes. The batter for the fritters can be prepared ahead of time, but the fritters should be served on a bed of salad greens as soon as they are done. To prevent the cheese from breaking out of its coating, make sure the oil is very hot—almost smoking—before lowering the fritters into the oil. The fritters go well with Joel Robuchon's Fresh Pea and Fava Bean Soup (page 50), serving the fritters, followed by the soup.

**For the Fritter Batter:**

1 egg

¹/₃ cup all-purpose flour

¹/₄ teaspoon salt

1 tablespoon vegetable oil

¹/₃ cup tepid beer

**For the Cheese:**

¹/₂ pound goat cheese

2 garlic cloves, mashed to a purée

¹/₂ teaspoon finely cracked black peppercorns

1 teaspoon minced fresh thyme leaves

2 tablespoons olive oil

Salt

¹/₂ pound watercress (1 bunch), thick stems cut off, washed, and spun-dry

¹/₄ pound arugula (1 bunch), thick stems cut off, washed, and spun-dry

3 cups corn oil

¹/₄ cup Vinaigrette Dressing (page 135)

**The batter:** Separate the egg. In the bowl of a heavy-duty mixer, beat the flour, egg yolk, salt, oil, and beer at low speed until smooth. Set aside.

**The cheese:** Discard the rind of the goat cheese if there is any and crumble the cheese. In the bowl of a food processor fitted with the steel blade, purée the cheese, garlic, peppercorns, thyme, and oil. Taste for seasoning, adding salt if necessary. Shape the cheese into 1-inch balls. Freeze for 1 hour.

**The fritters:** Beat the egg white until firm and fold it into the reserved batter. Before deep-frying the fritters, toss the greens in the dressing and place decoratively on a serving platter.

Heat the corn oil to 325 degrees in a deep-fryer. Working quickly, dip half the frozen cheese balls into the batter, coating them well. With a large spoon, gently lower them into the hot oil. Fry the cheese balls, turning them in the hot oil until the fritters are light golden. (Do not leave them too long or the cheese will escape and make a mess of the oil.) Scoop them out with the fine-meshed strainer and drain on a cake rack fitted over a large plate.

Reheat the oil to 325 degrees and repeat with the second batch of fritters.

Dribble the vinaigrette over the salad greens and garnish with the fritters. Serve right away.

# red beet salad in a lemon and walnut oil dressing

Buy small quantities of walnut oil because it becomes rancid quickly; keep the bottle in the refrigerator to prolong its life. This salad goes well with Spanish Black Bean Soup (page 81).

2 pounds red beets

1 tablespoon white vinegar

3 tablespoons fresh lemon juice

2 teaspoons grated lemon rind

2 garlic cloves, peeled and mashed

1/4 cup walnut oil

2 tablespoons red wine vinegar

1 medium onion, peeled and thinly sliced (1 cup)

1/2 cup chopped walnuts

1/4 cup minced parsley

Salt

Freshly ground black pepper

Trim the stems from the beets and wash, being sure not to tear the skins. In a 6-quart pot, cover the beets with water and the white vinegar. (When the beets are cooked in their skins with white vinegar, they bleed less.) Bring to a boil; cover, reduce the heat, and simmer for 45 minutes or until the beets are barely tender. Drain the beets and cool, then peel them.

Combine the lemon juice, lemon rind, garlic, walnut oil, and vinegar in a large mixing bowl.

Cut the beets into slices or cubes. Toss them in the dressing along with the onion, walnuts, and parsley. Sprinkle with salt and pepper to taste.

**NOTE:** This is a salad that can keep a week in the refrigerator if necessary.

# salad greens with fried potatoes and onions

Dinner in most French farmhouses is eaten at noon, which means eating meat as one of the courses; suppers are often vegetarian with a soup and salad like this one.

I boil the potatoes at least 1 hour before supper and let them drain thoroughly before frying them. Cooked potatoes absorb less oil than raw potatoes.

1 1/2 pounds Yukon Gold potatoes

1/2 pound small onions, peeled and quartered (2 cups)

Vegetable oil, for frying

Salt

Freshly ground black pepper

8 cups loosely packed Boston lettuce (1 head), washed and spun-dry

1/4 cup Vinaigrette Dressing or more (page 135)

Scrub the potatoes under cold running water. Do not peel them. Cut the potatoes into 1-inch cubes (2 1/2 cups).

In a 4-quart pan, cover the potatoes with salted cold water. Bring to a boil, cover, reduce the heat, and simmer for 15 minutes or until the potatoes are tender. Drain thoroughly, leaving the potatoes in the strainer for at least 15 minutes, then pat dry with a tea towel. This step is important to prevent the oil from splattering when you fry the potatoes.

Fifteen minutes before dinner, pour about 1 inch of vegetable oil into each of two large skillets. Heat the oil and test the temperature by putting one potato cube in the oil—it should sizzle. When the oil is hot, gently lower the potatoes and onions into the hot fat in several batches with a fine-meshed skimmer (the hot oil will boil furiously). Fry for 10 minutes or until the potatoes turn golden.

Scoop out the potatoes and onions with the skimmer in several batches, shaking the skimmer to drain off as much oil as possible (if you dry them with paper towels, the potatoes get mushy) and transfer them to a platter. Sprinkle with salt and freshly ground pepper.

Toss the lettuce greens with the potatoes and onions in the vinaigrette. Serve immediately.

# a lettuce salad with stuffed tomatoes

I stuff tomatoes with leftover meat from making Beef Broth (page 2). I divide the meat into 1-pound packages and freeze them. I also use this meat for Wayne Marshall's Tossed Salad (page 136). These tomatoes are best at room temperature with a chicory salad served after one of the cold soups.

12 (5-ounce) tomatoes

Salt

1 pound leftover beef, defrosted

1 medium onion,
peeled and coarsely chopped (1 cup)

3 large garlic cloves, peeled and coarsely chopped

Several sprigs of fresh flat-leaf parsley

Several sprigs of fresh thyme

Freshly ground black pepper

1/4 cup olive oil

8 cups loosely packed chicory or frisée leaves,
washed and spun-dry

1/2 cup Vinaigrette Dressing (page 135)

Cut a 1/2-inch-thick slice from each tomato, opposite the stem end. With a grapefruit spoon, scoop out the pulp and chop it. Reserve.

Salt the inside of each tomato and prick the flesh so the tomato will not burst while cooking. Place them upside down with their respective hats on top. Let drain on a baking rack.

Meanwhile, grind the beef, onion, garlic, parsley, and thyme. Combine in a bowl with the tomato pulp and sprinkle with 1 tablespoon salt and pepper.

In a large nonstick skillet, heat the oil and brown the meat mixture for about 10 minutes, stirring once in a while.

Preheat the oven to 400 degrees.

Overfill each tomato and top it with a hat. Drizzle a little olive oil in a 3-quart baking dish and place the tomatoes in it. Drizzle more over the top.

Bake in the middle of the oven for about 1 hour. Drain the liquid that will spew out of the tomatoes into a small sauce pan. Boil the liquid down until slightly syrupy, then dribble the syrup over the tomatoes and let cool. (These tomatoes can be prepared a day or two ahead of time; bring them back to room temperature before dinnertime.)

Just before serving, toss the chicory with the vinaigrette and garnish a platter, first with the greens, then the tomatoes.

# monkfish and exotic mushrooms on mesclun

Mesclun is a mixture of young salad greens. You can make your own mesclun salad with watercress, baby Boston lettuce, arugula, dandelion greens, radicchio, basil, and so on. I suggest serving Takishamaya Pea and Snow Pea Soup (page 52) before this salad.

**For the Monkfish:**

1 1/2 pounds monkfish fillets

1 tablespoon whole black peppercorns, crushed

1/2 teaspoon salt

3 tablespoons olive oil

1 1/2 tablespoons minced shallots

1/2 cup white wine

4 tablespoons (1/4 cup) butter

**For the Mushrooms:**

1 tablespoon olive oil

1/4 pound shiitake mushrooms, rinsed, stems removed, and quartered

1 tablespoon minced parsley

Salt

Freshly ground black pepper

8 loose cups salad leaves, washed and spun-dry

1/4 cup or more Vinaigrette Dressing (page 135)

**The monkfish:** Dip the fish fillets in the pepper. Sprinkle with salt.

In a large nonstick skillet, heat the olive oil and sauté the fillets for 2 minutes on each side. Add the shallots and wine, and cover; lower the heat and braise for another 5 minutes. Transfer the fish to a carving board and cool for 5 minutes before cutting into nuggets. Reserve on a serving platter.

Turn the heat to high under the skillet and boil down the wine until the liquid reduces by half. Reduce the heat and whisk in the butter, 1 tablespoon at a time. You should have a syrupy butter sauce. Pour the sauce into a sauceboat.

**The mushrooms:** In a large skillet, heat 1 tablespoon oil and stir-fry the mushrooms with the parsley for 2 minutes or until the mushrooms start to color. Season with salt. Add the mushrooms to the fish.

In a large mixing bowl, toss the greens in the dressing. Garnish the platter with the salad greens around the fish. Serve immediately along with the butter sauce. Pour the sauce over each serving of fish surrounded by the greens.

# shrimp salad

For a pleasant summer luncheon on my terrace, I sometimes choose a cold soup like the Guatemalan Avocado Soup (page 60), followed by the shrimp salad, and for dessert, an Apricot Clafoutis (page 187).

2 pounds medium shrimp

¼ cup vegetable oil

1 medium tomato, chopped

1 cup white wine, such as Chardonnay

Salt

1 cup water

½ cup heavy cream

3 tablespoons minced fresh tarragon

Red pepper flakes

8 cups loosely packed red leaf lettuce (1 head), washed and spun-dry

¼ cup Vinaigrette Dressing (page 135)

Shell the shrimp and reserve the shells. With a small sharp knife, slit the back of each shrimp lengthwise and remove the vein.

Heat the vegetable oil in a large nonstick skillet. Add the shrimp shells and stir-fry until they turn pink. Add the tomato, wine, salt, and water. Bring to a boil, cover, reduce the heat, and simmer for 10 minutes. Add the cream and 2 tablespoons of the minced tarragon. Simmer for another 10 minutes.

Strain the sauce through a fine-mesh sieve over a bowl. Press on the shells to extract all the liquid; discard the solids. Reduce the sauce if necessary to a slightly syrupy consistency. Reserve in a sauce boat.

In the same large skillet, heat the remaining 2 tablespoons vegetable oil over high heat and stir-fry the shrimps in several batches. Season with salt and red pepper flakes to taste and reserve on a serving platter.

In a large bowl, toss the salad greens in the vinaigrette. Taste and correct seasoning. Garnish the shrimp platter with the greens and serve right away. Pass the tarragon sauce at the table and have each guest ladle sauce over the shrimp.

# a salad of foie gras and fruit over watercress

During the Christmas holidays, I serve this salad with a bowl of Squash Soup (page 154) and Bread Rolls (page 33) for festive brunches. This is a recipe where the cook can add more of one of the ingredients or substitute different fruits.

1 pound fresh foie gras

Salt

Freshly ground pepper

2 tablespoons red wine vinegar

1 pineapple, peeled, cored and cut into 1-inch wedges

4 teaspoons sugar

2 cups black grapes, halved

2 large shallots, grated

3 tablespoons olive oil

2 bunches watercress, tough stems removed, washed and spun-dry

Toast (page 160)

Place the foie gras in a large bowl of cold water for a half hour.

Drain and detach the two lobes and remove the small blood vessels if any.

Cut the foie gras in $1/2$-inch-thick slices, sprinkle with salt and freshly ground pepper. Reserve on a plate.

Heat a large nonstick skillet, sauté the foie gras on both sides on very high heat for less than a minute on each side; the foie gras will melt considerably. After each batch, drain and reserve the excess fat. Transfer the foie gras to a plate and reserve.

Over high heat, pour the vinegar into the skillet and scrape the bottom of the pan and bring to a boil. Pour the boiling vinegar over the foie gras.

In the same skillet with 1 tablespoon or so of the melted fat, add the pineapple wedges. Sprinkle 1 tablespoon sugar and sauté until slightly caramelized. Reserve on a plate.

Still in the same skillet, add the grapes. Sprinkle with 1 teaspoon sugar and sauté until slightly caramelized. Reserve with the sautéed pineapple.

Mix the grated shallots with the olive oil in a salad bowl and toss in the watercress.

Decorate each plate with watercress and add foie gras and fruit on top. Dribble the vinegar and fruit juices that gathered in the plates over the foie gras. Serve with toast.

# fresh cranberry beans and calamari salad

This is my interpretation of a fabulous fresh bean and squid salad I had at Cantinetti Antoniori in Florence, years ago. I serve it with Cold Summer Squash Soup (page 62) or the Vichyssoise (page 63) for a luncheon or a light supper, followed by Taillevent's Fruit Gratin (page 185). If you can't find fresh cranberry beans, substitute 3 cups soaked and parboiled dried navy or cannellini beans.

3 cups shelled fresh cranberry beans

3 cups Chicken Broth (page 3),
Vegetable Broth (page 5), or a commercial broth
or bouillon cubes or more

2 large garlic cloves, chopped

Sea salt

Freshly ground black pepper

1/2 red onion, thinly sliced (1/2 cup)

4 tablespoons extra-virgin olive oil

1 pound calamari,
cleaned and sliced into 1/4-inch rings

2 red bell peppers

Very fruity olive oil, to drizzle

In a 6-quart heavy-bottomed pot, combine the beans, broth, and garlic. Bring to a boil, cover, reduce the heat, and simmer for 1 to 1 1/2 hours or until the beans are very tender. Season the beans with salt and pepper toward the end of the cooking time. Check once in a while to be sure there is always broth in the pot; to avoid scorching the beans, add more broth if necessary. When the beans are cooked, the broth should be mostly evaporated.

Transfer the beans to a large serving bowl, add the raw onion slices, and toss them with 2 tablespoons olive oil while the beans are still hot. Reserve.

Meanwhile, put the peppers on top of a gas burner at medium heat, turning them once in a while with tongs until they are all charred. Transfer them to a mixing bowl and cover them with a plastic bag to cool.

Then quarter the peppers and discard the seeds and ribs. Cut each pepper quarter into 1-inch-thick slices, then again crosswise into 1-inch pieces. Toss them with the beans and onions. Reserve.

Slice the squid into 1-inch-thick rings and turn them inside out. In a large nonstick skillet, heat the remaining 2 tablespoons olive oil and stir-fry the squid in batches for 1 minute; season with salt and pepper. Toss the squid with the beans, peppers, and onions. Taste the salad and correct seasoning if necessary.

Serve the bean and squid salad with a small pitcher of olive oil; each guest can drizzle olive oil on his or her salad.

# breads

I enjoy making bread with my heavy-duty standing mixer. It's always ready to do the hard work while I prepare dinner.

I buy active dry yeast in bulk in health food stores; it's generally better quality than what you find in supermarkets. Yeast keeps well in the freezer. I also buy good-quality flour; the better the flour, the better the bread will be. Buy flour with 12 percent protein, if you can. The protein content should be given on the bag.

In winter, you will need more water and more yeast than in summer because winters are dry and flour absorbs more water.

Warm the bowl in which you are going to knead the dough by pouring boiling water into it; heat helps the bread to rise. Try making bread in a warm place; let it rise on top of a warm radiator, for example.

# 7

The breads in this chapter are my favorites for croutons, toasts, and sandwiches made with leftover meat or poultry from the Broth chapter. When I was testing Joe Ortiz's Tuscan Bread recipe for Ribollita (page 89) and Pappa al Pomodoro (page 17), I fell in love with the bread—after over a month of making it every three days, Wayne asked if the bread repertoire could change.

There's such satisfaction making one's own bread that I can only urge you to try if you have never been tempted before.

# bread rolls

I like making rolls when I serve soup for a dinner party. These rolls are very basic: flour, yeast, and water. I use an all-purpose flour with 12 percent gluten content and sometimes I substitute 1/2 cup whole wheat flour for 1 cup white flour.

3 1/4 cups warm water

1 tablespoon active dry yeast

1 teaspoon sugar

1 tablespoon salt

7–8 cups all-purpose flour

Cornmeal

Olive oil

Warm the bowl of a heavy-duty mixer by rinsing it with boiling water. Pour in 1/4 cup warm water, then sprinkle the yeast and sugar over the water. Let stand in a warm place for 5 minutes or until the mixture bubbles. Pour the remaining 3 cups warm water over the sponge. Sprinkle the salt over the flour and mix.

Fit the mixer with the paddle attachment or dough hook, and on its lowest speed, gradually add the flour, 1/4 cup at a time. When the dough becomes too stiff to knead in the machine, transfer it to a work surface sprinkled with flour. Knead the dough by hand until the dough is smooth.

Cut the dough into two pieces. Transfer the dough in two large oiled bowls. (The dough will rise so much that just one large bowl might not be big enough.) Clip the top of the dough with scissors, cover with plastic bags, creating a tent. Place them in a warm place to double in bulk.

Gently punch the dough down, cover once more with bags, and refrigerate overnight or at least for 4 hours.

Flour the work surface, knead the dough 1 minute, and cut each piece into 8-inch pieces roughly for the rolls or cut the number of rolls you want and refrigerate the remaining dough for another day.

Preheat the oven to 425 degrees.

Sprinkle cornmeal on a cookie sheet. Place the rolls on it, leaving space for them to expand. Brush olive oil over them. Slash the top with scissors and let them rise for 30 minutes. Bake for about 30 minutes or until the bottoms are slightly colored. Cool at room temperature. They'll keep several days wrapped in a plastic bag.

# poilane bread

The Poilane family makes the most famous sourdough bread in Paris. Many Parisian hostesses keep Poilane bread in the freezer, just in case. It's an excellent bread, great for sandwiches as well as for making croutons.

**For the Starter:**

1 cup all-purpose flour

1/3 cup spring water

1 teaspoon active dry yeast

**For the Bread:**

1 1/2 cups warm water

2 teaspoons active dry yeast

1/2 cup whole wheat flour

Several cups all-purpose flour

1 tablespoon salt

**The starter:** Rinse the bowl of a heavy-duty mixer with boiling water. Mix the flour, water, and yeast in the bowl. Cover with a plastic bag and keep for three days next to a radiator during the winter or on a kitchen table for two days during summer. The starter will sour and bubble slightly.

**The bread:** Add the warm water and yeast to the starter. At the lowest speed of a standing mixer fitted with the paddle attachment or dough hook, beat the mixture. Gradually beat in 1/4 cup flour at a time, starting with the whole wheat flour; continue with the all-purpose flour mixed with the salt. Stop adding flour when the dough is gathered around the paddle or dough hook and it comes clean off the bowl in a mass.

Sprinkle flour on a work surface and transfer the dough. Continue kneading by hand, adding flour as necessary to make a light spongy dough. Transfer the dough to a large bowl, cover with a plastic bag, and let rise until doubled in bulk.

Again, knead the dough on a work surface dusted with flour, adding more flour until the dough becomes elastic but not dry.

Before shaping the dough into a round loaf, cut off roughly the equivalent of 2 cups of dough; that will be the starter for your next bread. Put the starter in a 6-cup plastic measuring cup and cover tightly with aluminum foil. Refrigerate until ready to make more bread, generally within ten days. (If you don't intend to make more bread within the ten days, knead $1/2$ cup flour into the starter. A day before making the bread, remove the starter from the refrigerator to bring it back to room temperature and follow the instructions for making sourdough bread.)

Shape the dough into a perfect ball and place in a heavily floured cloth-lined basket. Cover with a plastic bag and keep in a warm place until the dough has risen to $1\,1/2$ times its original volume; depending on many factors such as time of year, humidity, the warmth of your kitchen, it can take from 2 to 4 hours.

Preheat the oven to 400 degrees.

Place a baking stone in the middle of the oven to heat. Flour the baking stone and turn the bread basket upside down on the hot stone. Slash diamond-shape designs on the top of the bread with the point of a knife. Bake 1 hour or so or until golden.

Transfer the bread to a cake rack and cool completely inside a plastic bag to soften the crust.

# poilane's rye and nut bread

Rye flour

$1/2$ cup whole wheat flour

1 cup chopped pecans

Substitute rye flour for the white flour in making the bread and add 1 cup chopped pecans.

# tuscan bread

Tuscan bread is made without salt even today, though salt is no longer taxed as it was in the Middle Ages. A drizzle of very fruity olive oil over a slice of Tuscan bread, plus a sprinkle of salt, is a lovely treat. When the bread is stale, make Ribollita (page 89) or Pappa al Pomodoro (page 17). To make this bread, I was inspired by Joe Ortiz's instructions in his bread book, *The Village's Baker,* with great results. Now I make Tuscan bread at least once a month. There are three steps to making this bread: First, some of the flour is mixed with boiling water and put to rest for as long as twenty-four hours; then the yeast and warm water are added to make a sponge, and finally the remaining flour is incorporated. So plan ahead.

6 cups all-purpose flour

1 3/4 cups boiling water

1 package active dry yeast (about 1 tablespoon)

1 1/2 cups warm water

**First day:** Put 2 cups of flour in the bowl of a heavy-duty mixer with the paddle attachment, beat in the boiling water at low speed until the flour is totally wet. Cover the bowl with a large plastic bag and let stand for 10 hours or overnight.

**Second day:** Mix the yeast with the warm water. When the mixture is creamy, beat it into the reserved flour-water mixture. At low speed, add the remaining 4 cups flour, 1/4 cup at a time. It takes about 15 minutes to incorporate most of the flour. If the dough gets too stiff to incorporate by machine, turn the dough out onto a worktable and knead with your hands for 5 minutes or until all the flour is incorporated and the dough is very smooth. Transfer the dough to a large bowl. Cover it with a plastic bag and let it rise in a warm place until doubled in size—depending on the weather, from 1 to 2 hours.

Dust flour on the worktable and knead the dough for 1 minute. Gather the sides of the dough to the middle. Flour your hands and flatten it; it will be the shape of an irregular round loaf. Cover with a plastic bag. Let it rise for 30 minutes.

Preheat the oven to 400 degrees.

Once more, flatten the dough with floured hands and flip it over onto a baking sheet dusted with flour. Cover and let rise again for 30 minutes.

Bake the bread in the middle shelf of the oven for 45 to 50 minutes. Turn off the oven and leave the loaf in the oven for another 5 minutes to develop a golden crust.

Transfer the bread to a cooling rack. Wrap it in a tea towel and keep several days.

# bread for toasting

This bread is very simple to make. It has only one rising and can be kept frozen, already sliced. Toasts and croutons are great with soups.

1 tablespoon active dry yeast

2 1/4 cups lukewarm water

1 teaspoon sugar

5–5 1/2 cups unbleached all-purpose flour

1/2 cup whole wheat flour

1 tablespoon salt

Butter

In the bowl of a heavy-duty mixer, sprinkle the yeast over 1/4 cup of warm water; stir in the sugar. Let stand until foamy, about 5 minutes.

Add the remaining 2 cups warm water, then with the paddle attachment, first gradually beat in the all-purpose flour, about 1/4 cup at a time at low speed, then continue with the whole wheat flour mixed with the salt.

Turn the dough out onto a floured surface and knead for a minute, until the dough is smooth and silky to the touch. Cut the dough into two equal pieces; shape each piece into a sausage shape. Put the dough into two well-buttered 6-cup loaf pans, preferably black tin. Cover the pans with plastic wrap, set in a warm place, and let stand until the dough has risen three-fourths of the way up the sides of the pans, about 1 hour.

Preheat the oven to 400 degrees. Bake the loaves until they are golden, about 30 minutes.

Unmold onto a rack and let cool for about 1 hour before slicing.

For toasts, turn the broiler on. Brush olive oil on one side of the bread slices. Place them, brushed side up, on a cookie sheet. Place in the middle rack of the oven for about 3 minutes or so until the bread is lightly golden on one side, checking almost every minute.

# croutons

My husband is the crouton maker in our family for all the soups he eats! He devised a sure way to make perfect croutons in the oven.

6 ounces two-day-old bread

3 tablespoons olive oil

Turn the broiler to high.

Cut the bread into $1/2$-inch slices, then cube it.

Pour the olive oil into a cast-iron or nonstick skillet that can go into the oven or line a cookie sheet with aluminum foil. Toss the bread in the oil.

Place the skillet or cookie sheet 3 inches beneath the heating element and broil for 5 to 6 minutes or so until the bread is golden brown, checking almost every minute, and tossing the cubes so they brown evenly. They are better made when you need them; they take no time at all to make, but if you have to make them ahead of time, reheat them for 5 minutes in a 300-degree oven.

# potato flat bread

This bread resembles a focaccia.

1 large baking potato (about $1/2$ pound),
not peeled

Salt

$1/4$ cup milk

2 teaspoons active dry yeast

$1/2$ teaspoon sugar

$1 1/2$ cups all-purpose flour

1 large egg

3 tablespoons very fruity olive oil or melted butter

Sea salt, for sprinkling

**First day:** In a medium saucepan, cover the potato with cold water, add salt, and bring to a boil over high heat. Reduce the heat and simmer until the potato is tender, about 30 minutes.

Place $1/4$ cup of the tepid potato cooking water in a medium bowl. Stir the milk, yeast, and sugar into the potato water and let stand until foamy, about 5 minutes.

Peel the potato. Quickly pass the potato through a ricer or beat in a heavy-duty standing mixer. Let cool.

Combine the flour and 1 teaspoon salt. Beat the yeast mixture into the cooled mashed potato along with the egg. Gradually beat in the flour mixture until smooth (the mixture will be more like batter than dough). Cover the bowl and let stand until the dough doubles in bulk, about 1 hour.

Deflate the dough with a wooden spoon, cover, and refrigerate overnight.

**Second day:** Oil a 9 by 13-inch rimmed baking sheet. Using your hands, spread the cold dough evenly over the sheet. Let stand until the dough has doubled, 30 to 40 minutes.

Preheat the oven to 375 degrees.

Drizzle the olive oil or brush melted butter over the bread and sprinkle with sea salt. Bake for 25 minutes or until golden.

Cut into wedges and serve right away, or if you have to bake the bread during the day for the evening, reheat it in a 300-degree oven for 10 minutes.

# flour tortillas

For years I kept this recipe in a folder, knowing that one day I might make these.

1 ¹/₂ cups all-purpose flour

¹/₂ tablespoon baking powder

1 teaspoon salt

2 tablespoons solid vegetable shortening

About ³/₄ cup water

**Hand method:** In a large bowl, combine the flour, baking powder, salt, and shortening and mix with your hands until the shortening is absorbed. Gradually, add the water and mix thoroughly until the dough forms. Knead like bread for about 3 minutes. Let stand 30 minutes.

**Mixer method:** Fit a heavy-duty mixer with the flat paddle or dough hook. Combine the flour, baking powder, salt, and shortening in the mixing bowl. Beat at medium speed until the shortening is absorbed, then gradually add the water and continue mixing until the dough makes a ball. Knead by hand for a minute or so. Let stand 30 minutes.

**To finish:** On a floured surface, using 1 tablespoon of dough at a time, roll out very thin to a free-form 6-inch circle or cut out a perfect circle (called *pastale* in Spanish) by placing a 6-inch plate over the dough. Make more *pastales* with the trimmings.

**To cook the tortillas whole:** Heat a 9-inch nonstick skillet (I use it without any fat). Cook the tortilla one minute on each side.

**To fry tortillas for chips:** Cut the tortillas into 1-inch strips. Heat about 1 inch of vegetable oil in a skillet. Fry the strips to golden brown, turning once. Drain on paper towels.

# pullman bread

This is a fine-textured white bread baked in a tightly covered loaf pan. When the bread is cooked, it has no crust, which makes it ideal for finger sandwiches or fruit puddings or buttered toasts. A pullman bread pan is rectangular with a top that slides closed.

**For the Sponge:**

3/4 cup warm milk

1 tablespoon active dry yeast

1 teaspoon sugar

1 1/2 cups all-purpose flour

**For the Bread:**

2 teaspoons salt

2 1/2 cups all-purpose flour

1 cup warm milk

6 tablespoons unsalted butter + 1 teaspoon to grease the mold

**The sponge:** Rinse the bowl of a heavy-duty standing mixer with boiling water. Combine the milk, yeast, and sugar in the bowl. On medium speed, with the dough hook or paddle attachment, gradually beat in the flour. Cover with a plastic bag and let it rest for at least 15 minutes in a warm place.

**The bread:** Add the salt to the flour. On low speed, beat the milk into the sponge. Raise the speed to medium and alternate adding butter and flour, beating the mixture until the dough is very smooth. Cover the dough and let rise in a warm place until it has doubled in size.

Grease the loaf pans with butter. Flour your hands and knead the bread very briefly. Cut it in half and fill each pan halfway. Cover with plastic bags. It should take no more than 30 minutes in warm weather, or a little more in winter—again, the loaves can be put in an oven which was turned on to low and then turned off. Let rise to the rim of the pans. Cover with aluminum foil and weight down with something heavy—bricks or a heavy pan if you don't have a pullman bread pan with a slide-in cover.

Preheat the oven to 425 degrees.

Bake in the middle of the oven for 40 minutes. Cool, then remove the weights and peel off the paper, taking care to keep rising steam away from your face.

Wait several hours before slicing the loaves. Only slice the amount needed. Wrap the remaining loaves in plastic and refrigerate.

# quick pizza

The following dough is made and cooked within two hours. The dough is rolled out just like a short crust dough, very thin with no additional rise before baking. If you like a thin crackling crust on your pizza, this one is for you.

**For the Pizza Dough:**

2 cups all-purpose flour

2 teaspoons active dry yeast

3/4 cup warm water

3 tablespoons olive oil

1/3 teaspoon salt

**For the Tomato Topping:**

3 tablespoons olive oil

1 small onion, peeled and thinly sliced (1/2 cup)

1 (28-ounce) can crushed Italian tomatoes

1 teaspoon sugar

Salt

Freshly ground black pepper

1 tablespoon tomato paste

**For the Assembly:**

3 cups grated Gruyère cheese

1 tablespoon dried oregano

12 pitted black olives

Olive oil, to drizzle

**The dough:** In the bowl of a heavy-duty mixer fitted with the paddle attachment, combine the flour, the yeast mixed with the warm water, the olive oil, and salt. Beat at low speed until the mixture is totally combined. (Depending on the flour you use, weather, etc., you might need another half tablespoon or so of water to combine the dough.) Knead by hand for 1 minute or so to smooth out the dough (the dough should be a bit sticky). Transfer it to a plate, clip the top with a pair of scissors, and cover it with a damp kitchen towel or a plastic bag from the supermarket. Keep in a warm place for 45 minutes or until it almost doubles in bulk.

**The tomato topping:** Heat the olive oil in a large nonstick skillet and cook the onion until it starts coloring to a tawny yellow. Add the tomatoes, and crush them into the onion with a spoon. Sprinkle with sugar, salt, and pepper. Mix the tomato paste with 1/2 cup of tomato liquid from the can and add to the mixture. Cover, reduce the heat, and simmer for 15 minutes. Uncover, raise the heat, and continue cooking for a minute or so until the tomato mixture is the consistency of a relish. Cool.

**The assembly:** Roll out the dough very thin. Line an oiled 14 by 17-inch cookie sheet with the dough and trim it to fit. (Reserve the trimmings and roll them out for an individual pizza.) Prick the dough all over with the tines of a fork.

Preheat the oven to 425 degrees.

Spread the tomato topping (reserve some for the trimmings) evenly over the dough, sprinkle with the cheese and oregano, and garnish with the olives in four rows, three for each row. Drizzle more olive oil over the pizza. Bake for 15 minutes or until the bottom of the dough is golden. Serve immediately.

# pan bagnat
## tuna fish sandwich from the french riviera

*Pan bagnat* literally means "bread taking a bath." Years ago, dried leftover crusty bread was soaked in water to be used again for sandwiches like *pan bagnat* or to make soup like the Ribollita (page 89) and Pappa al Pomodoro (page 17).

*Pan bagnat* originates in Nice on the French Riviera, where I had one of my sources find the authentic *pan bagnat* for Calvin Trillin, who wrote about it for *Gourmet* magazine (February 2001). "It's a tunafish hamburger," said Judy, a friend who was part of the *pan bagnat* search team. Indeed it is—a large roll stuffed with salad greens, onion, and shallot marinated in lots of olive oil, tuna, tomato, hard-boiled egg, anchovy, radishes, and olives, all layered in this scrumptious sandwich.

Very often, we have a soup and this sandwich for dinner; in the fall, I serve Pan Bagnat after a Porcini Consommé (page 23), or after the Classic French Leek and Potato Soup (page 14). Traditionally *pan bagnat* is made with a roll, but choose the bread you like. You could make it with Kaiser Rolls, homemade (page 170) or store-bought also, but if you can't find them, try a hero roll (remove the doughy center and make bread crumbs with them). Remember, the bread needs to be soaked with all the oil and ingredients. You can prepare it in advance but do not refrigerate.

1 large onion, minced (1 cup)

1 shallot, minced

1/2 cup olive oil, or more as needed

1 tablespoon wine vinegar

6 ounces canned tuna in olive oil

2 tablespoons lemon juice

2 teaspoons salt

Freshly ground black pepper

4 Kaiser Rolls (page 170) or
hero rolls (store-bought)

4 lettuce leaves mixture of oak leaf lettuce,
Boston lettuce, shredded

2 large fresh tomatoes, thinly sliced

2 hard-boiled eggs, sliced

8 anchovy fillets

Several large radishes, sliced

Several black olives, pitted

In a large bowl, stir the onion and shallot in 6 tablespoons of the olive oil and the vinegar. Add the tuna with some of the olive oil from the cans and sprinkle over the lemon juice. Add 1 teaspoon salt and the pepper; with your hands, work the tuna with the onion and shallot until very well mixed. Marinate overnight or at least 1 hour or so.

Cut the rolls in half crosswise and place the halves on four individual plates. Drizzle the remaining 2 tablespoons oil all over the cut sides of the bread. Cover the bottom halves of the rolls with salad greens, then layer the ingredients in the following order: tomato slices, tuna-onion mixture, hard-boiled egg slices, 2 anchovy fillets crisscrossed, and the radishes and olives. Season with the remaining teaspoon salt and more pepper. Drizzle more olive oil on top. Cover with the top halves of the rolls, pressing gently on them. Let the sandwiches marinate for an hour or so.

# kaiser rolls for pan bagnat

Here is a kaiser roll recipe for those who cannot find them in a store. This is a simplified recipe from *The Home Baker,* by Joe Ortiz.

**For the Sponge:**

1 1/2 teaspoons active dry yeast

1/4 cup warm water

1/2 cup warm milk

1/2 cup tap water

2 teaspoons sugar

1/2 teaspoon honey

1 1/2 cups all-purpose flour

**Finishing the Dough:**

1 1/2 teaspoons salt

1 cup all-purpose flour

Poppy seeds

**Making the sponge:** In the bowl of a heavy-duty mixer, add the yeast and warm water. When the mixture is creamy, beat in the milk, tap water, sugar, and honey at low speed. Gradually beat in 1 1/2 cups of flour. Cover the bowl with a plastic bag and wait till the sponge has doubled; depending on the weather, it might take 1 to 2 hours.

Mix the salt in the remaining flour. Gradually beat the flour into the risen sponge; add more flour if the dough is too sticky. Scrape the dough off the bowl onto a floured surface and knead until dough is very smooth (about 2 to 3 minutes). Let the dough rise in a greased bowl, covered with a plastic bag (about 1 to 2 hours).

Divide the dough into six pieces on a floured surface. Make a ball of each piece. Then flatten each ball with the palm of the hand.

Place the rolls on a cookie sheet lined with parchment paper. Brush vegetable oil over them. Cover them again with parchment paper. Put another cookie sheet on top of the rolls and then a skillet to weigh down the dough. Don't worry, it flattens the dough, which is fine. Let rise for another 35 minutes. The dough will have spread and kept the top flat.

Preheat the oven to 450 degrees.

Remove the skillet, cookie sheet, and top parchment paper. Brush the rolls lightly with water and sprinkle them with poppy seeds.

Spray water in the oven and bake the rolls on the middle rack for 20 minutes or until golden. Spray water 2 or 3 times while the rolls are cooking. Cool on a baking rack. Wrap in plastic bag until needed.

# sandwich monte cristo

I remember making this sandwich the first year I came to the United States many years ago from France. I arrived at Thanksgiving and my aunt had invited Monsieur Camille, a French chef from one of Cleveland's restaurants, who gave us this marvelous recipe for using leftover turkey. The days after Thanksgiving are named "turkey week" in my family, with soups made with the carcass and meat (see Turkey Broth (page 4) and this version of turkey *croque monsieur*. Traditionally, the Monte Cristo is soaked in cream; I have substituted milk for the sake of our waistlines and for health reasons.

1 teaspoon Dijon mustard or more

8 slices 1/4 inch thick of stale bread with very dense texture, such as Poilane Bread (page 156) or Tuscan Bread (page 158)

4 thin slices prosciutto

4 thin slices Gruyère cheese

4 leftover turkey breast slices

1 egg yolk

1 cup milk (whole, 2%, or 1%)

3 tablespoons butter or olive oil

Spread the mustard on each slice of bread. Build a sandwich with one layer each of prosciutto, cheese, and leftover turkey, then add salt, pepper, and one more slice of bread. Combine the egg yolk and milk in a large deep plate, like a soup plate. Dip the sandwiches in the milk mixture. If the bread is very stale and dense, leave it in the mixture for 5 minutes to soften and soak up the milk.

Melt the butter or heat the oil in a 12-inch skillet. Brown the sandwiches on both sides. Cover the skillet, reduce the heat, and cook for another 2 to 3 minutes to be sure the cheese melts. Serve with a soup.

# chapter

# desserts

As a child I loved custards, perhaps because it was such a treat to find eggs, butter, and milk during World War II. Even today, caramelized custards, puddings, and crepes are still my favorite desserts. Nowadays, I sometimes use fruit to garnish the custards, a delicacy unavailable during the war. In fact, the first time I was given an orange, I bit into it just like an apple!

Fruit and custard desserts, like simple fruit tarts, complement a meal of soup and salad, and they are homey and comforting, like the meal that precedes them.

# 8

# meringue cookies

Electric ovens are best for making meringues, as it's difficult to keep the meringues pristine in a gas oven. I don't expect you to buy a special oven for meringues, so if your oven is gas, watch the meringues carefully as they bake. Turn the oven off once in a while during the baking so the temperature doesn't exceed 190 degrees. The heat in a gas oven is not as steady as in an electric oven—that's my experience.

The meringue cookies are good as is, but even better with whipped lemon cream sandwiched between two meringues.

**For the Cookies:**

1/2 cup egg whites

1 cup superfine sugar

**For the Filling:**

1/2 cup heavy cream

1 tablespoon sugar

1 teaspoon finely grated lemon zest

Preheat the oven to 190 degrees. Place two racks straddling the center of the oven. Line two cookie sheets with parchment paper.

**The cookies:** In the bowl of a heavy-duty standing mixer fitted with the whisk attachment, beat the egg whites at high speed until they are stiff and dry. If you turn the bowl upside down, the meringue should stick to the bowl.

Still at full speed, gradually add 1 heaping tablespoon of sugar at a time, waiting a minute between adding the next. It takes about 10 minutes. The egg whites with all the sugar incorporated should be very dense and shiny.

Scoop half the meringue at a time into a large pastry bag fitted with a 1/2-inch nozzle. Hold the nozzle with one hand and with the other hand, squeeze the meringue out of the bag, keeping it perpendicular to the cookie sheet and about $1/2$ inch away from the parchment paper. Shape thick lady fingers (3 by 1 inch), coils, or just round blobs. You need to work quickly—the sugar in the meringue wets the pastry bag, making it sticky to handle. Repeat with the second half of meringue mixture.

Bake for 1 hour.

Turn off the oven and leave the meringues in the oven until cool. Store the meringues in a covered plastic container.

**The filling:** Beat the cream until thick, then beat in the sugar and the lemon zest. Make a sandwich with two meringues, filled with the flavored whipped cream.

# raspberry soup

My friend Harvey S. Shipley Miller, a philanthropist and patron of the arts, frequently entertains. One of his favorite summer desserts is this raspberry soup that he learned to make from Rosella, his family's cook.

We tested the soup in cooking class, and it was a unanimous thumbs up. I served the soup with meringue cookies crumbled on top—it was delicious.

2 pints fresh raspberries

3 ripe freestone peaches (about 1 pound), peeled, pitted, and cut into pieces

1/4 cup granulated sugar

1/4 cup honey

8 ounces plain yogurt

2 tablespoons sour cream

1/4 cup milk

1 large sprig of fresh mint

Meringue Cookies (page 174–75), optional

In a large bowl, mix the raspberries and peaches with the sugar and honey. Purée the mixture in a blender, processing it in three batches.

Fold in the yogurt and sour cream.

Strain the soup through a fine-meshed sieve to discard the raspberry seeds.

Thin the soup with milk to the consistency you like.

Bury a large sprig of fresh mint in the soup. Refrigerate until well chilled.

Discard the mint. Serve in chilled glass bowls. If desired, crumble meringue cookies on top.

# strawberry soup scented with fresh mint

In the spring and summer, I serve berry soups for very refreshing desserts. To add flavor to the soup, I marinate fresh herbs in it for at least twenty-four hours. I accompany the soup with cookies, and if I have not used cream in the menu, I serve a bowl of sweetened sour cream or crème fraîche.

**For the Soup:**

1 1/4 pounds strawberries

3 tablespoons sugar

**For the Syrup:**

1/2 cup water

1/2 cup sugar

1 teaspoon fresh lemon juice

3 branches of fresh mint

A bowl of sweetened sour cream or crème fraîche (optional)

**The soup:** Put the strawberries in a large fine-meshed sieve and quickly rinse them under cold running water. Drain completely and pat dry with paper towels.

Hull the strawberries. Cut several strawberries into slices, enough to make 1 cup. Sprinkle the sugar over them and reserve in a pretty serving bowl. Place the remaining strawberries in the bowl of a food processor and process until liquefied. Set aside.

**The syrup:** Bring the water and sugar to a boil and boil for 3 minutes. Let cool.

Whisk the sugar syrup and the lemon juice into the strawberry soup. Pour the strawberry soup over the reserved strawberries and bury the fresh mint in it. Cover and refrigerate for at least 24 hours.

Discard the mint and, if desired, serve with a bowl of sweetened sour cream (sweeten it to your taste) or crème fraîche and cookies.

# mrs. marshall's brown sugar ice box cookies

There is a *Mrs. Marshall's Larger Cookery Book of Extra Recipes* with lots of cookies, one of the numerous books Mrs. Marshall wrote in the late nineteenth century. In my family, Mrs. Marshall's cookies are the ones that my mother-in-law made for so many years to the delight of her children, grandchildren, and great-grandchildren.

8 tablespoons ($^{1}/_{2}$ cup) unsalted butter

$^{1}/_{2}$ cup dark brown sugar

1 cup all-purpose flour

$^{1}/_{2}$ teaspoon baking soda

$^{1}/_{2}$ teaspoon water

Pinch of salt

Butter

**Combine all the ingredients in the bowl of a food processor fitted with the metal blade. Process for 30 seconds or until smooth.**

**Dust a work surface with flour and roll out the dough into a 3-inch-thick cylinder. Wrap it in waxed paper and refrigerate overnight.**

**Preheat the oven to 350 degrees. Butter two cookie sheets.**

**Cut the batter into $^{1}/_{8}$-inch-thick slices and bake on the buttered cookie sheets for 8 to 10 minutes or until golden brown. Cool on a rack.**

**NOTE:** You don't have to bake all the cookies at once. I bake only enough for a day or two and reserve the remaining dough in the freezer, and I defrost the dough just enough to slice the cookies without crumbling.

# vanilla cream with prunes soaked in brandy

*Crème anglaise,* as the French call this custard, makes a lovely dessert soup, especially with the addition of prunes or other brandy-soaked fruit.

1/3 cup superfine sugar

2 1/2 cups milk

1 tablespoon vanilla extract

6 egg yolks

1 teaspoon cornstarch (optional)

10 Prunes Soaked in Brandy (page 180) or several Cherries in Brandy (page 181)

Bring the sugar and milk to a boil. Turn off the heat, add the vanilla extract, and cover the pan. Let sit 15 to 30 minutes.

In a large heavy-bottomed pan, whisk the egg yolks (add the cornstarch if you are nervous about the egg yolks curdling; it will stabilize them). Pour the cooled sweetened milk into the pan and whisk briskly to incorporate the yolks in the milk. Cook the mixture over low heat, stirring and scraping the bottom and sides of the pan with a wooden spatula to cook it evenly. It takes 15 to 20 minutes or so in a heavy-bottomed copper pan, less in a lighter pan. Have a large bowl of ice water next to the stove to stop the cooking, if necessary. If the mixture starts to thicken in 5 minutes, it's going too fast and will curdle.

The vanilla cream is ready when it lightly coats the spoon and is the consistency of a thin eggnog. Turn off the heat but do not stop stirring. Plunge the pan into the ice water to stop cooking the cream and to lower the temperature of the pan, especially if the pan is copper.

Add the prunes or other fruits, quartered, to the cream. Refrigerate until ready to eat. It can be kept for about four days, refrigerated.

# prunes soaked in brandy or port

The prunes are good as a quick and easy dessert on their own, and delicious with yogurt or vanilla ice cream. The prunes can be used overnight or they can be kept almost indefinitely. As you use the prunes, you can add more to the jar, but push them to the bottom so you eat the prunes that have been marinating longest.

3 dozen prunes with their pits

2 strips of dried orange peel

Several tablespoons brandy or port

Fill the jar with the prunes and pack them in tightly. Add the orange peel and enough brandy or port to cover the prunes. Keeps up to one year.

# cherries in brandy

Cherries, like prunes, are delicious marinated in brandy; however, they are better soaked in a mixture of brandy and sugar syrup, as I find the alcohol alone masks the cherry flavor. I always have jars of cherries with their stems on in the refrigerator, and when I feel like one, I catch a cherry on its stem and eat it as is.

About 60 large ripe cherries with their stems on

4 tablespoons granulated sugar

Several tablespoons brandy

Prick the cherries all over with a needle and pack into the jar, layered with 4 rounded tablespoons of sugar. Cover with the brandy and seal the jar, making sure that it is air-tight (if not, keep in the refrigerator).

Leave to mature for at least four months. Other alcohol may be used, but it must be at least 80 proof.

# crepes like my mother used to make

My mother never measured anything. I don't think she owned a scale, and she never used a cookbook, yet she was known as an excellent cook. I lost her when I was fifteen, just after World War II. During the war we had no ingredients, but for Mardi Gras she would always find eggs and milk for crepes, my favorite dessert. I was too young to think of writing everything down, and I lost the taste of her crepes until one day, not long ago, I visited my cooking neighbor, Colette, who had just made crepes and they tasted like my mother's. We had a feast, spreading jam and sprinkling sugar over them. But Colette, like my mother, never measures, so I came equipped with measuring cups and tablespoons.

1 ¹/₂ cups all-purpose flour

¹/₄ teaspoon salt

1 tablespoon sugar

6 medium to large eggs

1 cup + 2 tablespoons milk

1 tablespoon dark rum

Solid vegetable shortening, for greasing the skillet

In a large bowl, mix the flour, salt, and sugar. Crack the eggs on top of the flour. Start whisking the eggs and flour, then pour the milk into the eggs and whisk until smooth. Add the rum. You can also combine the ingredients in the bowl of a heavy-duty standing mixer fitted with the paddle attachment. Beat until smooth. Cover and set aside for no longer than 1 hour at room temperature.

Grease the bottom of a 10-inch nonstick skillet lightly with shortening. Heat the skillet until hot. Whisk the crepe batter and pour about 3 tablespoons into the center of the skillet. Quickly tilt the pan around, spreading the batter to cover the bottom of the skillet. Use a light plastic spatula to spread the batter evenly. Cook for 1 minute. The crepe is very thin; use the spatula or your hands to flip over the crepe and cook for another minute or until the bottom is very lightly golden.

Stack the crepes on a plate as you make them. It takes about 45 minutes to cook all the crepes. Cover them with another plate and reheat to warm in a microwave or on top of simmering water.

To serve, sprinkle sugar or spread jam on the crepes and roll them like a cigarette.

# caramelized bread pudding

The Pullman Bread on page 164 is perfect for this dessert, as well as for the Raspberry and Blueberry Pudding (page 190)

**For the Caramel:**

¹/₂ cup superfine sugar

3 tablespoons water

**For the Pudding:**

¹/₂ cup skinned whole almonds

1 cup milk

2 cups soft bread torn without the crust into small pieces, loosely packed

¹/₃ cup granulated sugar

6 tablespoons unsalted butter, softened

3 eggs, separated

6 Prunes Soaked in Brandy (page 180), pitted and quartered

Sabayon (page 184)

**The caramel:** Combine the sugar and water in an enameled or unlined copper saucepan. Bring the syrup to a boil, stirring with a wooden spoon to dissolve the sugar. As soon as the boil is reached, stop stirring. Continue boiling until the syrup caramelizes, about 8 minutes.

Pour the hot caramel into a 4-cup ring mold, holding the mold with pot holders. As best as you can swirl the caramel against the sides of the mold. When the caramel starts to cool, brush it all over the inside of the mold. Set aside.

**The pudding:** Grind the almonds in a rotary cheese grater.

Bring the milk to a boil. Turn off the heat and mash the crumbled bread into the milk with a fork. Add the sugar and mix. Continue mixing while adding the butter, egg yolks, and almonds. Fold the prunes into the bread mixture.

Preheat the oven to 350 degrees.

In a heavy-duty mixer fitted with the whisk attachment, beat the egg whites until firm. With a rubber spatula, fold the egg whites into the bread mixture. Ladle the pudding into the prepared ring mold. Place the mold into a larger pan filled with enough boiling water to come halfway up the mold. Bake on the middle shelf of the oven for 45 minutes. Cover loosely with foil after 30 minutes to avoid burning.

Unmold the pudding onto a platter. Serve warm with the sabayon.

# sabayon

Sabayon, or zabaglione, can be made into a dessert of its own or it can be served warm, over puddings.

1/2 cup sugar

3 egg yolks

1/3 cup dry white wine

1/4 cup grated lemon peel

In the mixing bowl of a heavy-duty mixer fitted with the whisk, beat the sugar and egg yolks until very thick and pale yellow, about 10 minutes.

Transfer it to the top of a double boiler over simmering water (or a large saucepan set into another bigger pan filled halfway with simmering water). Beat in the wine and the lemon zest, and whisk briskly over low heat until the sabayon thickens, about 10 minutes.

Serve immediately with pudding.

# taillevent's fruit gratin

These delicious individual fruit gratins were on the menu during the week I spent in the kitchen at Taillevent, the renowned Paris restaurant.

**For the Pastry Cream:**

1 1/2 tablespoons cornstarch

1 1/2 tablespoons all-purpose flour

1/3 cup sugar

1 cup milk

2 large egg yolks

2 tablespoons unsalted butter, cut up

1 tablespoon Cointreau liqueur

**For the Fruits:**

1 small pineapple, peeled, cored, and cut into 1-inch chunks

1 pint strawberries, quartered

3/4 cup sugar

2/3 cup crème fraîche

**The pastry cream:** Sift together the cornstarch and the flour; whisk in the sugar.

Bring the milk to a boil and pour half the boiling milk into the flour-sugar mixture, whisking briskly. Quickly whisk in the egg yolks, then pour the mixture into the remaining milk in the pan. Over medium heat, whisk until the mixture is very thick. Remove the pan from the heat and whisk in the butter and liqueur until very smooth. Cool and reserve.

**The fruits:** Toss the fruits with 1/4 cup of the sugar in a bowl.

Combine the pastry cream and crème fraîche with a whisk. Keep refrigerated.

Divide half the fruit among six buttered 1/2-cup ramekins. Set aside. (Can be done several hours ahead of time up to this step.)

Preheat the broiler and set a rack 4 inches from the heat.

Before serving, spoon the cream mixture over the fruit and top with the remaining 1/2 cup sugar. Broil until bubbly and lightly golden, 4 minutes or so. Cool for 20 minutes and serve with cookies.

# cherry clafoutis

Traditionally, clafoutis was baked with unpitted cherries in a thick custard. Nowadays, other fruits are put in—cherries, figs, and apricots are my favorite fruits for clafoutis. Also, I prefer to pit the cherries so the cherry juice mixes with the custard.

2 pounds ripe black cherries, pitted (2 1/2 cups)

1/2 cup all-purpose flour

3 eggs

1/2 cup sugar

1/2 cup heavy cream

1/2 cup milk

Preheat the oven to 350 degrees. Layer the cherries in a greased 3-quart glass baking pan.

In a medium mixing bowl, whisk the flour, eggs, sugar, cream, and milk together. Pour the mixture over the cherries and bake for 30 minutes in the middle of the oven or until golden brown.

Serve at room temperature.

# apricot clafoutis

Apricots become very tart when they are baked and need much more sugar than cherries.

1 cup sugar

4 eggs

4 tablespoons melted butter

$^2/_3$ cup all-purpose flour

1 cup milk

1 $^1/_2$ pounds apricots, pitted and quartered

Preheat the oven to 350 degrees.

In the mixing bowl of a heavy-duty mixer, beat $^3/_4$ cup sugar with the eggs until thick and pale yellow, about 10 minutes. Drizzle in the melted butter and gradually beat in the flour. Slowly, whisk in the milk.

Layer the apricots in a greased 3-quart glass baking dish and pour the batter over them. Bake in the middle of the oven for 45 minutes or until golden brown.

Dust the clafoutis with the remaining sugar and serve at room temperature.

# apple galette

This is a simple free-form apple tart made with a short crust. I jazz up the meal with this tart for a family dinner of soup and salad when Wayne invites people to share our dinner on the spur of the moment.

1 cup all-purpose flour

Pinch of salt

8 tablespoons cold butter, cut into small pieces

4 tablespoons cold water

2 Golden or Granny Smith apples (1 pound)

1/4 cup melted apple jelly or more

Several dots of butter

Sugar to sprinkle

A bowl of sweetened sour cream

In a food processor fitted with the steel blade, combine the flour, salt, and butter. Process for 10 seconds. Sprinkle the water over the flour-butter mixture and process another 10 seconds.

Dump the mixture onto a work surface and quickly bind it with the palm of your hand into a ball. Sprinkle flour on the ball and flatten it into a 5-inch-diameter disk. Refrigerate for 30 minutes.

Peel the apples, then quarter and slice them as thin as possible.

Preheat the oven to 400 degrees.

Sprinkle a little flour on a work surface and on a rolling pin and roll out the dough into a large 16-inch circle. Be sure to flour the work surface under the dough and the rolling pin at all times to prevent the dough from sticking to the surface. Brush off the excess flour on top of the rolled out dough and fold in two. Brush off once more the excess flour, and fold into quarters. Again brush off the flour on the top and bottom.

Unfold the dough onto a 14 x 17-inch cookie sheet. Overlap the apple slices starting from 1 inch within the circle edge, making a ring, then continue overlapping the apples within the ring to the center of the dough. Each row of apples should overlap by a quarter the length of each apple slice.

Fold the 1-inch edge over the first row of apples. Brush the melted apple jelly over the top of the dough and on all the apples. Dot tiny pieces of butter over the apples and sprinkle on some sugar. Bake on the middle rack for 30 minutes or until the top is slightly caramelized. Serve warm with a bowl of sweetened sour cream.

# raspberry and blueberry pudding

This pudding is a variation on a summer English pudding made with berries and bread. I make mostly with store-bought lady fingers or brioche, but you could use leftover Pullman Bread.

When the berries are plentiful during the summer, this pudding is my favorite dessert for guests.

1 cup sugar

1 cup water

8 cups raspberries

4 cups blueberries

1 tablespoon Chambord liqueur
or raspberry brandy

About 18 lady fingers or 1 pound brioche
store-bought or Pullman Bread
(page 164), cut into 1/2-inch slices

A bowl of sweetened sour cream or crème fraîche

Combine the sugar and water in a large pan. Add 4 cups of berries and bring to a boil. When the liquid is at a rolling boil, scoop out the berries with a slotted spoon and transfer them to a fine-meshed strainer placed over a mixing bowl. Continue with the remaining berries until all have been poached in the syrup.

Boil down the syrup to about 1 1/2 cups, occasionally adding the liquid that accumulates in the bowl under the berries. Add the liqueur to the syrup and reserve 1/2 cup of the syrup for later. Mix the berries with the remaining syrup.

Line a buttered 2-quart glass dish with lady fingers or slices of brioche and sprinkle the reserved 1/2 cup syrup over them. Spoon the berries over the soaked lady fingers or cakes. Chill.

Serve the pudding with either sweetened sour cream or crème fraîche.

# warm chocolate tortes

This is a chocolate mousse baked in ring molds and served warm with sweetened crème fraîche or sour cream. The center of the tortes should stay creamy at the end of baking, but it's a little tricky to know exactly when to remove them from the oven. I have always found individual ovens to be capricious; it's a trial-and-error experience, but once you have mastered the timing, this delicious, easy dessert will be in your repertoire.

Valrhona is my favorite chocolate, which is made in the valley of the Rhône—hence the name—in Tain L'Hermitage, a little town better known for its wines than its chocolate!

¹/₄ pound bittersweet Valrhona chocolate

4 tablespoons unsalted butter

4 large eggs, separated

6 tablespoons sugar

A bowl of crème fraîche or sweetened sour cream

Butter and flour the inside of eight 3-inch ring molds and place them on a cookie sheet. Reserve.

Cut the chocolate into small pieces and melt with the butter in the top of a double boiler. Cool the chocolate.

Meanwhile, beat the egg whites until firm, gradually adding the sugar.

Combine the chocolate mixture and the beaten egg whites. Ladle the chocolate mousse into the prepared molds. Refrigerate until needed. (Can be done a day ahead of time.)

Preheat the oven to 400 degrees.

Bake the molds for 8 to 10 minutes. Transfer the tortes in their rings to individual plates with a pie server. Serve with crème fraîche or sour cream.

# index